SELECTIONS FROM THE GREEK ELEGIAC, IAMBIC AND LYRIC POETS

LONDON : GEOFFREY CUMBERLEGE
OXFORD UNIVERSITY PRESS

SELECTIONS
from the
GREEK ELEGIAC, IAMBIC
and
LYRIC POETS

BY

J. A. MOORE

JUNIOR FELLOW OF THE SOCIETY OF FELLOWS
OF HARVARD UNIVERSITY

HARVARD UNIVERSITY PRESS

CAMBRIDGE, MASSACHUSETTS

1947

55979

881.08

M 822 s

PREFACE

THIS book is essentially a revision of *Selections from the Elegiac, Iambic, and Lyric Poets for the Use of Students in Harvard University*, originally made by H. M. Morgan, and revised by C. B. Gulick. I have added some poems to that selection and omitted others. I have departed more freely than Professor Gulick from the text of Diehl's *Anthologia Lyrica* (though I have used it as my guide), taking some readings from Wilamowitz, some from Bowra, some from Lobel, some from other sources; two were suggested to me by Professor Werner Jaeger, none is my own. The numbering of the fragments is that of Diehl's 1925 edition.

In writing the notes I have tried to be accurate and helpful, and to be brief without being sphinxlike. I owe a great deal to Professor Gulick's notes, which I have kept open before me. I am indebted to Wilamowitz' *Sappho und Simonides*, and most heavily indebted to C. M. Bowra's two illuminating books, *Early Greek Elegists* and *Greek Lyric Poetry*. My notes are full of his interpretations; I could not acknowledge them severally (for to do so would have involved me in notes on notes), but I wish to acknowledge them inclusively here.

Professors Jaeger, Post, Whatmough, and Greene of this university have most kindly and helpfully discussed with me various problems which arose. I wish to thank the Society of Fellows for affording me the leisure to prepare this book, and to express my deep gratitude to Professor J. H. Finley for the abundant assistance which he has unstintingly given me.

J. A. MOORE.

October, 1946.

ERRATA

SOLON
p. 13, frag. 22, l. 3: for Διγναστάδη read Λιγναστάδη

XENOPHANES
p. 16, frag. 30, l. 1: omit comma after ἔσται

THEOGNIS
p. 17, l. 78: for καλεπῇ read χαλεπῇ
p. 18, l. 214: insert period after ἔχει
p. 18, l. 215: for πέτρη read πέτρῃ
p. 18, l. 217: for ἀλλοῖς read ἀλλοῖος

ARCHILOCHUS
p. 21, frag. 18, l. 4: for ἀμφι read ἀμφὶ

STESICHORUS
p. 24, frag. 6, l. 2: for Ὠκεανοῖο read Ὠκεανοῖο
p. 24, frag. 6, l. 3: for ἀφίκοιθ read ἀφίκοιθ'

ALCAEUS
p. 25, frag. 2, l. 3: for Κρονίδα read Κρονίδᾳ

SAPPHO
p. 34, frag. 123, l. 5: for γάμβος read γάμβρος
p. 34, frag. 127, l. 1: for τίω read τίῳ

IBYCUS
p. 36, frag. 7, l. 1: for ὑπο read ὑπό

SIMONIDES
p. 39, frag. 4, l. 33: for φιγόμωμος read φιλόμωμος
p. 41, frag. 84, l. 2: for οἷ read οἱ'

SELECTIONS

from the

GREEK ELEGIAC, IAMBIC

and

LYRIC POETS

CALLINUS

I

Μέχρις τεῦ κατάκεισθε; κότ᾽ ἄλκιμον ἕξετε θυμόν,
 ὦ νέοι; οὐδ᾽ αἰδεῖσθ᾽ ἀμφιπερικτίονας
ὧδε λίην μεθιέντες; ἐν εἰρήνῃ δὲ δοκεῖτε
 ἧσθαι, ἀτὰρ πόλεμος γαῖαν ἅπασαν ἔχει.

. . . .

καί τις ἀποθνῄσκων ὕστατ᾽ ἀκοντισάτω.   5
τιμῆέν τε γάρ ἐστι καὶ ἀγλαὸν ἀνδρὶ μάχεσθαι
 γῆς πέρι καὶ παίδων κουριδίης τ᾽ ἀλόχου
δυσμενέσιν· θάνατος δὲ τότ᾽ ἔσσεται, ὁππότε κεν δή
 Μοῖραι ἐπικλώσωσ᾽· ἀλλά τις ἰθὺς ἴτω
ἔγχος ἀνασχόμενος καὶ ὑπ᾽ ἀσπίδος ἄλκιμον ἦτορ   10
 ἔλσας, τὸ πρῶτον μειγνυμένου πολέμου.
οὐ γάρ κως θάνατόν γε φυγεῖν εἱμαρμένον ἐστίν
 ἄνδρ᾽, οὐδ᾽ εἰ προγόνων ᾖ γένος ἀθανάτων.
πολλάκι δηϊοτῆτα φυγὼν καὶ δοῦπον ἀκόντων
 ἔρχεται, ἐν δ᾽ οἴκῳ μοῖρα κίχεν θανάτου·   15
ἀλλ᾽ ὁ μὲν οὐκ ἔμπης δήμῳ φίλος οὐδὲ ποθεινός,
 τὸν δ᾽ ὀλίγος στενάχει καὶ μέγας, ἤν τι πάθῃ·

λαῷ γὰρ σύμπαντι πόθος κρατερόφρονος ἀνδρός
   θνήσκοντος, ζώων δ᾿ ἄξιος ἡμιθέων·
ὥσπερ γάρ μιν πύργον ἐν ὀφθαλμοῖσιν ὁρῶσιν·   20
   ἔρδει γὰρ πολλῶν ἄξια μοῦνος ἐών.

TYRTAEUS

2

Αὐτὸς γὰρ Κρονίων, καλλιστεφάνου πόσις Ἥρης,
   Ζεὺς Ἡρακλείδαις τήνδε δέδωκε πόλιν·
οἷσιν ἅμα προλιπόντες Ἐρινεὸν ἠνεμόεντα
   εὐρεῖαν Πέλοπος νῆσον ἀφικόμεθα.

6, 7

Τεθνάμεναι γὰρ καλὸν ἐνὶ προμάχοισι πεσόντα
   ἄνδρ᾿ ἀγαθὸν περὶ ᾗ πατρίδι μαρνάμενον.
τὴν δ᾿ αὑτοῦ προλιπόντα πόλιν καὶ πίονας ἀγρούς
   πτωχεύειν πάντων ἔστ᾿ ἀνιηρότατον,
πλαζόμενον σὺν μητρὶ φίλῃ καὶ πατρὶ γέροντι   5
   παισί τε σὺν μικροῖς κουριδίῃ τ᾿ ἀλόχῳ.
ἐχθρὸς μὲν γὰρ τοῖσι μετέσσεται οὕς κεν ἵκηται
   χρησμοσύνῃ τ᾿ εἴκων καὶ στυγερῇ πενίῃ,
αἰσχύνει τε γένος, κατὰ δ᾿ ἀγλαὸν εἶδος ἐλέγχει,
   πᾶσα δ᾿ ἀτιμίη καὶ κακότης ἕπεται.   10
εἰ δ᾿ οὕτως ἀνδρός τοι ἀλωμένου οὐδεμί᾿ ὤρη
   γίγνεται οὔτ᾿ αἰδὼς οὐδ᾿ ὀπίσω γένεος,
θυμῷ γῆς πέρι τῆσδε μαχώμεθα καὶ περὶ παίδων
   θνήσκωμεν ψυχέων μηκέτι φειδόμενοι.
ὦ νέοι, ἀλλὰ μάχεσθε παρ᾿ ἀλλήλοισι μένοντες   15
   μηδὲ φυγῆς αἰσχρῆς ἄρχετε μηδὲ φόβου,
ἀλλὰ μέγαν ποιεῖσθε καὶ ἄλκιμον ἐν φρεσὶ θυμόν
   μηδὲ φιλοψυχεῖτ᾿ ἀνδράσι μαρνάμενοι·
τοὺς δὲ παλαιοτέρους, ὧν οὐκέτι γούνατ᾿ ἐλαφρά,
   μὴ καταλείποντες φεύγετε, τοὺς γεραιούς.   20

αἰσχρὸν γὰρ δὴ τοῦτο μετὰ προμάχοισι πεσόντα
κεῖσθαι πρόσθε νέων ἄνδρα παλαιότερον,
ἤδη λευκὸν ἔχοντα κάρη πολιόν τε γένειον,
θυμὸν ἀποπνείοντ᾽ ἄλκιμον ἐν κονίῃ,
αἱματόεντ᾽ αἰδοῖα φίλαις ἐν χερσὶν ἔχοντα —   25
αἰσχρὰ τά γ᾽ ὀφθαλμοῖς καὶ νεμεσητὸν ἰδεῖν —
καὶ χρόα γυμνωθέντα· νέοισι δὲ πάντ᾽ ἐπέοικεν,
ὄφρ᾽ ἐρατῆς ἥβης ἀγλαὸν ἄνθος ἔχῃ·
ἀνδράσι μὲν θηητὸς ἰδεῖν, ἐρατὸς δὲ γυναιξίν,
ζωὸς ἐών, καλὸς δ᾽ ἐν προμάχοισι πεσών·   30
ἀλλά τις εὖ διαβὰς μενέτω ποσὶν ἀμφοτέροισιν
στηριχθεὶς ἐπὶ γῆς, χεῖλος ὀδοῦσι δακών.

8

Ἀλλ᾽ — Ἡρακλῆος γὰρ ἀνικήτου γένος ἐστέ —
θαρσεῖτ᾽ — οὔπω Ζεὺς αὐχένα λοξὸν ἔχει —
μηδ᾽ ἀνδρῶν πληθὺν δειμαίνετε μηδὲ φοβεῖσθε,
ἰθὺς δ᾽ ἐς προμάχους ἀσπίδ᾽ ἀνὴρ ἐχέτω,
ἐχθρὴν μὲν ψυχὴν θέμενος, θανάτου δὲ μελαίνας   5
κῆρας ὁμῶς αὐγαῖς ἠελίοιο φίλας.
ἴστε γὰρ ὡς Ἄρεος πολυδακρύου ἔργ᾽ ἀίδηλα·
εὖ δ᾽ ὀργὴν ἐδάητ᾽ ἀργαλέου πολέμου
καὶ μετὰ φευγόντων τε διωκόντων τ᾽ ἐγένεσθε,
ὦ νέοι, ἀμφοτέρων δ᾽ ἐς κόρον ἠλάσατε.   10
οἳ μὲν γὰρ τολμῶσι παρ᾽ ἀλλήλοισι μένοντες
ἔς τ᾽ αὐτοσχεδίην καὶ προμάχους ἰέναι,
παυρότεροι θνήσκουσι, σαοῦσι δὲ λαὸν ὀπίσσω·
τρεσσάντων δ᾽ ἀνδρῶν πᾶσ᾽ ἀπόλωλ᾽ ἀρετή.
οὐδεὶς ἄν ποτε ταῦτα λέγων ἀνύσειεν ἕκαστα,   15
ὅσσ᾽, ἢν αἰσχρὰ πάθῃ, γίγνεται ἀνδρὶ κακά·
ἁρπαλέον γὰρ ὄπισθε μετάφρενόν ἐστι δαΐζειν
ἀνδρὸς φεύγοντος δηίῳ ἐν πολέμῳ·
αἰσχρὸς δ᾽ ἐστὶ νέκυς κακκείμενος ἐν κονίῃσι
νῶτον ὄπισθ᾽ αἰχμῇ δουρὸς ἐληλαμένος   20
ἀλλά τις εὖ διαβὰς μενέτω ποσὶν ἀμφοτέροισιν

στηριχθεὶς ἐπὶ γῆς, χεῖλος ὀδοῦσι δακών,
μηρούς τε κνήμας τε κάτω καὶ στέρνα καὶ ὤμους
    ἀσπίδος εὐρείης γαστρὶ καλυψάμενος·
δεξιτερῇ δ᾽ ἐν χειρὶ τινασσέτω ὄβριμον ἔγχος,   25
    κινείτω δὲ λόφον δεινὸν ὑπὲρ κεφαλῆς·
ἔρδων δ᾽ ὄβριμα ἔργα διδασκέσθω πολεμίζειν,
    μηδ᾽ ἐκτὸς βελέων ἑστάτω ἀσπίδ᾽ ἔχων,
ἀλλά τις ἐγγὺς ἰὼν αὐτοσχεδὸν ἔγχεϊ μακρῷ
    ἢ ξίφει οὐτάζων δήιον ἄνδρ᾽ ἑλέτω·   30
καὶ πόδα πὰρ ποδὶ θεὶς καὶ ἐπ᾽ ἀσπίδος ἀσπίδ᾽ ἐρείσας,
    ἐν δὲ λόφον τε λόφῳ καὶ κυνέην κυνέῃ
καὶ στέρνον στέρνῳ πεπλημένος ἀνδρὶ μαχέσθω,
    ἢ ξίφεος κώπην ἢ δόρυ μακρὸν ἑλών.
ὑμεῖς δ᾽, ὦ γυμνῆτες, ὑπ᾽ ἀσπίδος ἄλλοθεν ἄλλος   35
    πτώσσοντες μεγάλοις βάλλετε χερμαδίοις,
δούρασί τε ξεστοῖσιν ἀκοντίζοντες ἐς αὐτούς,
    τοῖσι πανόπλοισι πλησίον ἱστάμενοι.

9

Οὔτ᾽ ἂν μνησαίμην οὔτ᾽ ἐν λόγῳ ἄνδρα τιθείην
    οὔτε ποδῶν ἀρετῆς οὔτε παλαιμοσύνης,
οὐδ᾽ εἰ Κυκλώπων μὲν ἔχοι μέγεθός τε βίην τε,
    νικῴη δὲ θέων Θρηίκιον Βορέην,
οὐδ᾽ εἰ Τιθωνοῖο φυὴν χαριέστερος εἴη,   5
    πλουτοίη δὲ Μίδεω καὶ Κινύρεω μάλιον,
οὐδ᾽ εἰ Τανταλίδεω Πέλοπος βασιλεύτερος εἴη,
    γλῶσσαν δ᾽ Ἀδρήστου μειλιχόγηρυν ἔχοι,
οὐδ᾽ εἰ πᾶσαν ἔχοι δόξαν πλὴν θούριδος ἀλκῆς·
    οὐ γὰρ ἀνὴρ ἀγαθὸς γίγνεται ἐν πολέμῳ,   10
εἰ μὴ τετλαίη μὲν ὁρῶν φόνον αἱματόεντα
    καὶ δηίων ὀρέγοιτ᾽ ἐγγύθεν ἱστάμενος.
ἥδ᾽ ἀρετή, τόδ᾽ ἄεθλον ἐν ἀνθρώποισιν ἄριστον
    κάλλιστόν τε φέρειν γίγνεται ἀνδρὶ νέῳ.
ξυνὸν δ᾽ ἐσθλὸν τοῦτο πόληί τε παντί τε δήμῳ,   15
    ὅστις ἀνὴρ διαβὰς ἐν προμάχοισι μένῃ

νωλεμέως, αἰσχρῆς δὲ φυγῆς ἐπὶ πάγχυ λάθηται,
   ψυχὴν καὶ θυμὸν τλήμονα παρθέμενος,
θαρσύνῃ δ᾽ ἔπεσιν τὸν πλησίον ἄνδρα παρεστώς·
   οὗτος ἀνὴρ ἀγαθὸς γίγνεται ἐν πολέμῳ·   20
αἶψα δὲ δυσμενέων ἀνδρῶν ἔτρεψε φάλαγγας
   τρηχείας, σπουδῇ δ᾽ ἔσχεθε κῦμα μάχης.
ὅς δ᾽ αὖτ᾽ ἐν προμάχοισι πεσὼν φίλον ὤλεσε θυμόν
   ἄστυ τε καὶ λαοὺς καὶ πατέρ᾽ εὐκλεΐσας,
πολλὰ διὰ στέρνοιο καὶ ἀσπίδος ὀμφαλοέσσης   25
   καὶ διὰ θώρηκος πρόσθεν ἐληλαμένος,
τὸν δ᾽ ὀλοφύρονται μὲν ὁμῶς νέοι ἠδὲ γέροντες
   ἀργαλέῳ τε πόθῳ πᾶσα κέκηδε πόλις,
καὶ τύμβος καὶ παῖδες ἐν ἀνθρώποισ᾽ ἀρίσημοι
   καὶ παίδων παῖδες καὶ γένος ἐξοπίσω·   30
οὐδέ ποτε κλέος ἐσθλὸν ἀπόλλυται οὐδ᾽ ὄνομ᾽ αὐτοῦ,
   ἀλλ᾽ ὑπὸ γῆς περ ἐὼν γίγνεται ἀθάνατος,
ὅντιν᾽ ἀριστεύοντα μένοντά τε μαρνάμενόν τε
   γῆς πέρι καὶ παίδων θοῦρος Ἄρης ὀλέσῃ.
εἰ δὲ φύγῃ μὲν κῆρα τανηλεγέος θανάτοιο,   35
   νικήσας δ᾽ αἰχμῆς ἀγλαὸν εὖχος ἕλῃ,
πάντες μιν τιμῶσιν ὁμῶς νέοι ἠδὲ παλαιοί,
   πολλὰ δὲ τερπνὰ παθὼν ἔρχεται εἰς Ἀΐδην·
γηράσκων ἀστοῖσι μεταπρέπει, οὐδέ τις αὐτόν
   βλάπτειν οὔτ᾽ αἰδοῦς οὔτε δίκης ἐθέλει,   40
πάντες δ᾽ ἐν θώκοισιν ὁμῶς νέοι οἵ τε κατ᾽ αὐτόν
   εἴκουσ᾽ ἐκ χώρης οἵ τε παλαιότεροι.
ταύτης νῦν τις ἀνὴρ ἀρετῆς εἰς ἄκρον ἱκέσθαι
   πειράσθω θυμῷ, μὴ μεθιεὶς πολέμου.

MIMNERMUS

1

Τίς δὲ βίος, τί δὲ τερπνὸν ἄτερ χρυσῆς Ἀφροδίτης;
  τεθναίην, ὅτε μοι μηκέτι ταῦτα μέλοι,
κρυπταδίη φιλότης καὶ μείλιχα δῶρα καὶ εὐνή·
  οἶ᾽ ἥβης ἄνθεα γίγνεται ἁρπαλέα
ἀνδράσιν ἠδὲ γυναιξίν· ἐπεὶ δ᾽ ὀδυνηρὸν ἐπέλθῃ   5
  γῆρας, ὅ τ᾽ αἰσχρὸν ὁμῶς καὶ κακὸν ἄνδρα τιθεῖ,
αἰεί μιν φρένας ἀμφὶ κακαὶ τείρουσι μέριμναι,
  οὐδ᾽ αὐγὰς προσορῶν τέρπεται ἠελίου,
ἀλλ᾽ ἐχθρὸς μὲν παισίν, ἀτίμαστος δὲ γυναιξίν·
  οὕτως ἀργαλέον γῆρας ἔθηκε θεός.   10

2

Ἡμεῖς δ᾽ οἷά τε φύλλα φύει πολυάνθεμος ὥρη
  ἔαρος, ὅτ᾽ αἶψ᾽ αὐγῇσ᾽ αὔξεται ἠελίου,
τοῖσ᾽ ἴκελοι πήχυιον ἐπὶ χρόνον ἄνθεσιν ἥβης
  τερπόμεθα, πρὸς θεῶν εἰδότες οὔτε κακόν
οὔτ᾽ ἀγαθόν· Κῆρες δὲ παρεστήκασι μέλαιναι,   5
  ἡ μὲν ἔχουσα τέλος γήραος ἀργαλέου,
ἡ δ᾽ ἑτέρη θανάτοιο· μίνυνθα δὲ γίγνεται ἥβης
  καρπός, ὅσον τ᾽ ἐπὶ γῆν κίδναται ἠέλιος·
αὐτὰρ ἐπὴν δὴ τοῦτο τέλος παραμείψεται ὥρης,
  αὐτίκα δὴ τεθνάναι βέλτιον ἢ βίοτος·   10
πολλὰ γὰρ ἐν θυμῷ κακὰ γίγνεται· ἄλλοτε οἶκος
  τρυχοῦται, πενίης δ᾽ ἔργ᾽ ὀδυνηρὰ πέλει·
ἄλλος δ᾽ αὖ παίδων ἐπιδεύεται, ὧν τε μάλιστα
  ἱμείρων κατὰ γῆς ἔρχεται εἰς Ἀίδην·
ἄλλος νοῦσον ἔχει θυμοφθόρον· οὐδέ τις ἔστιν   15
  ἀνθρώπων ᾧ Ζεὺς μὴ κακὰ πολλὰ διδοῖ.

4

Τιθωνῷ μὲν ἔδωκεν ἔχειν κακὸν ἄφθιτον ὁ Ζεύς
  γῆρας, ὃ καὶ θανάτου ῥίγιον ἀργαλέου.

5

Αὐτίκα μοι κατὰ μὲν χροιὴν ῥέει ἄσπετος ἱδρώς,
  πτοιῶμαι δ᾽ ἐσορῶν ἄνθος ὁμηλικίης
τερπνὸν ὁμῶς καὶ καλόν, ἐπεὶ πλέον ὤφελεν εἶναι·
  ἀλλ᾽ ὀλιγοχρόνιον γίνεται ὥσπερ ὄναρ
ἥβη τιμήεσσα· τὸ δ᾽ οὐλόμενον καὶ ἄμορφον   5
  αὐτίχ᾽ ὑπὲρ κεφαλῆς γῆρας ὑπερκρέμαται.

6

Αἲ γὰρ ἄτερ νούσων τε καὶ ἀργαλέων μελεδωνέων
  ἑξηκονταέτη μοῖρα κίχοι θανάτου.

10

Ἥλιος μὲν γὰρ πόνον ἔλλαχεν ἤματα πάντα,
  οὐδέ κοτ᾽ ἄμπαυσις γίγνεται οὐδεμία
ἵπποισίν τε καὶ αὐτῷ, ἐπεὶ ῥοδοδάκτυλος Ἠώς
  Ὠκεανὸν προλιποῦσ᾽ οὐρανὸν εἰσαναβῇ·
τὸν μὲν γὰρ διὰ κῦμα φέρει πολυήρατος εὐνή   5
  κοίλη, Ἡφαίστου χερσὶν ἐληλαμένη
χρυσοῦ τιμήεντος, ὑπόπτερος, ἄκρον ἐφ᾽ ὕδωρ
  εὕδονθ᾽ ἁρπαλέως χώρου ἀφ᾽ Ἑσπερίδων
γαῖαν ἐς Αἰθιόπων, ἵνα δὴ θοὸν ἅρμα καὶ ἵπποι
  ἑστᾶσ᾽, ὄφρ᾽ Ἠὼς ἠριγένεια μόλῃ·   10
ἔνθ᾽ ἐπεβήσεθ᾽ ἑῶν ὀχέων Ὑπερίονος υἱός.

SOLON

I

Μνημοσύνης καὶ Ζηνὸς Ὀλυμπίου ἀγλαὰ τέκνα,
  Μοῦσαι Πιερίδες, κλῦτέ μοι εὐχομένῳ·
ὄλβον μοι πρὸς θεῶν μακάρων δότε καὶ πρὸς ἁπάντων
  ἀνθρώπων αἰεὶ δόξαν ἔχειν ἀγαθήν·
εἶναι δὲ γλυκὺν ὧδε φίλοισ᾽, ἐχθροῖσι δὲ πικρόν,   5
  τοῖσι μὲν αἰδοῖον, τοῖσι δὲ δεινὸν ἰδεῖν.

χρήματα δ' ἱμείρω μὲν ἔχειν, ἀδίκως δὲ πεπᾶσθαι
  οὐκ ἐθέλω· πάντως ὕστερον ἦλθε δίκη.
πλοῦτον δ' ὃν μὲν δῶσι θεοί, παραγίγνεται ἀνδρί
  ἔμπεδος ἐκ νεάτου πυθμένος ἐς κορυφήν·   10
ὃν δ' ἄνδρες μετίωσιν ὑφ' ὕβριος, οὐ κατὰ κόσμον
  ἔρχεται, ἀλλ' ἀδίκοισ' ἔργμασι πειθόμενος
οὐκ ἐθέλων ἕπεται, ταχέως δ' ἀναμίσγεται ἄτη·
  ἀρχὴ δ' ἐξ ὀλίγου γίγνεται ὥστε πυρός,
φλαύρη μὲν τὸ πρῶτον, ἀνιηρὴ δὲ τελευτᾷ·   15
  οὐ γὰρ δὴν θνητοῖσ' ὕβριος ἔργα πέλει.
ἀλλὰ Ζεὺς πάντων ἐφορᾷ τέλος, ἐξαπίνης δὲ
  ὥς τ' ἄνεμος νεφέλας αἶψα διεσκέδασεν
ἠρινός, ὃς πόντου πολυκύμονος ἀτρυγέτοιο
  πυθμένα κινήσας, γῆν κατὰ πυροφόρον   20
δῃώσας καλὰ ἔργα, θεῶν ἕδος αἰπὺν ἱκάνει
  οὐρανόν, αἰθρίην δ' αὖτις ἔθηκεν ἰδεῖν·
λάμπει δ' ἠελίοιο μένος κατὰ πίονα γαῖαν
  καλόν, ἀτὰρ νεφέων οὐδὲν ἔτ' ἔστιν ἰδεῖν·
τοιαύτη Ζηνὸς πέλεται τίσις, οὐδ' ἐφ' ἑκάστῳ   25
  ὥσπερ θνητὸς ἀνὴρ γίγνεται ὀξύχολος,
αἰεὶ δ' οὔ ἑ λέληθε διαμπερές, ὅστις ἀλιτρόν
  θυμὸν ἔχῃ, πάντως δ' ἐς τέλος ἐξεφάνη·
ἀλλ' ὁ μὲν αὐτίκ' ἔτεισεν, ὁ δ' ὕστερον· οἱ δὲ φύγωσιν
  αὐτοί, μηδὲ θεῶν μοῖρ' ἐπιοῦσα κίχῃ,   30
ἤλυθε πάντως αὖτις· ἀναίτιοι ἔργα τίνουσιν
  ἢ παῖδες τούτων ἢ γένος ἐξοπίσω.
θνητοὶ δ' ὧδε νοεῦμεν ὁμῶς ἀγαθός τε κακός τε
  εὖ δεινὴν αὐτὸς δόξαν ἕκαστος ἔχει,
πρίν τι παθεῖν· τότε δ' αὖτις ὀδύρεται· ἄχρι δὲ τούτου   35
  χάσκοντες κούφαις ἐλπίσι τερπόμεθα.
χὤστις μὲν νούσοισιν ὑπ' ἀργαλέῃσι πιεσθῇ,
  ὡς ὑγιὴς ἔσται, τοῦτο κατεφράσατο·
ἄλλος δειλὸς ἐὼν ἀγαθὸς δοκεῖ ἔμμεναι ἀνήρ,
  καὶ καλός, μορφὴν οὐ χαρίεσσαν ἔχων·   40
εἰ δέ τις ἀχρήμων, πενίης δέ μιν ἔργα βιᾶται,

κτήσεσθαι πάντως χρήματα πολλὰ δοκεῖ.
σπεύδει δ᾽ ἄλλοθεν ἄλλος· ὁ μὲν κατὰ πόντον ἀλᾶται
   ἐν νηυσὶν χρῄζων οἴκαδε κέρδος ἄγειν
ἰχθυόεντ᾽, ἀνέμοισι φορεύμενος ἀργαλέοισιν,   45
   φειδωλὴν ψυχῆς οὐδεμίαν θέμενος·
ἄλλος γῆν τέμνων πολυδένδρεον εἰς ἐνιαυτόν
   λατρεύει, τοῖσιν καμπύλ᾽ ἄροτρα μέλει·
ἄλλος Ἀθηναίης τε καὶ Ἡφαίστου πολυτέχνεω
   ἔργα δαεὶς χειροῖν ξυλλέγεται βίοτον,   50
ἄλλος Ὀλυμπιάδων Μουσέων πάρα δῶρα διδαχθείς,
   ἱμερτῆς σοφίης μέτρον ἐπιστάμενος·
ἄλλον μάντιν ἔθηκεν ἄναξ ἑκάεργος Ἀπόλλων,
   ἔγνω δ᾽ ἀνδρὶ κακὸν τηλόθεν ἐρχόμενον,
ᾧ συνομαρτήσωσι θεοί· τὰ δὲ μόρσιμα πάντως   55
   οὔτε τις οἰωνὸς ῥύσεται οὔθ᾽ ἱερά.
ἄλλοι Παιῶνος πολυφαρμάκου ἔργον ἔχοντες
   ἰητροί· καὶ τοῖσ᾽ οὐδὲν ἔπεστι τέλος·
πολλάκι δ᾽ ἐξ ὀλίγης ὀδύνης μέγα γίγνεται ἄλγος,
   κοὐκ ἄν τις λύσαιτ᾽ ἤπια φάρμακα δούς·   60
τὸν δὲ κακῶς νούσοισι κυκώμενον ἀργαλέῃσιν
   ἁψάμενος χειροῖν αἶψα τίθησ᾽ ὑγιῆ.
μοῖρα δέ τοι θνητοῖσι κακὸν φέρει ἠδὲ καὶ ἐσθλόν,
   δῶρα δ᾽ ἄφυκτα θεῶν γίγνεται ἀθανάτων.
πᾶσι δέ τοι κίνδυνος ἐπ᾽ ἔργμασιν, οὐδέ τις οἶδεν   65
   ἧ μέλλει σχήσειν χρήματος ἀρχομένου·
ἀλλ᾽ ὁ μὲν εὖ ἔρδειν πειρώμενος οὐ προνοήσας
   ἐς μεγάλην ἄτην καὶ χαλεπὴν ἔπεσεν,
τῷ δὲ κακῶς ἔρδοντι θεὸς περὶ πάντα δίδωσιν
   συντυχίην ἀγαθήν, ἔκλυσιν ἀφροσύνης.   70
πλούτου δ᾽ οὐδὲν τέρμα πεφασμένον ἀνδράσι κεῖται·
   οἳ γὰρ νῦν ἡμέων πλεῖστον ἔχουσι βίον,
διπλασίως σπεύδουσι· τίς ἂν κορέσειεν ἅπαντας;
   κέρδεά τοι θνητοῖσ᾽ ὤπασαν ἀθάνατοι,
ἄτη δ᾽ ἐξ αὐτῶν ἀναφαίνεται, ἣν ὁπότε Ζεύς   75
   πέμψῃ τεισομένην, ἄλλοτε ἄλλος ἔχει.

2

Αὐτὸς κήρυξ ἦλθον ἀφ' ἱμερτῆς Σαλαμῖνος,
κόσμον ἐπέων ᾠδὴν ἀντ' ἀγορῆς θέμενος.

.   .   .   .

εἴην δὴ τότ' ἐγὼ Φολεγάνδριος ἢ Σικινίτης
ἀντί γ' Ἀθηναίου πατρίδ' ἀμειψάμενος·
αἶψα γὰρ ἂν φάτις ἥδε μετ' ἀνθρώποισι γένοιτο·   5
' Ἀττικὸς οὗτος ἀνὴρ τῶν Σαλαμιναφετῶν.'

.   .   .   .

ἴομεν ἐς Σαλαμῖνα μαχησόμενοι περὶ νήσου
ἱμερτῆς χαλεπόν τ' αἶσχος ἀπωσόμενοι.

3

Ἡμετέρα δὲ πόλις κατὰ μὲν Διὸς οὔποτ' ὀλεῖται
αἶσαν καὶ μακάρων θεῶν φρένας ἀθανάτων·
τοίη γὰρ μεγάθυμος ἐπίσκοπος ὀβριμοπάτρη
Παλλὰς Ἀθηναίη χεῖρας ὕπερθεν ἔχει.
αὐτοὶ δὲ φθείρειν μεγάλην πόλιν ἀφραδίῃσιν   5
ἀστοὶ βούλονται χρήμασι πειθόμενοι,
δήμου θ' ἡγεμόνων ἄδικος νόος, οἷσιν ἑτοῖμον
ὕβριος ἐκ μεγάλης ἄλγεα πολλὰ παθεῖν·
οὐ γὰρ ἐπίστανται κατέχειν κόρον οὐδὲ παρούσας
εὐφροσύνας κοσμεῖν δαιτὸς ἐν ἡσυχίῃ.   10

.   .   .   .

πλουτοῦσιν δ' ἀδίκοισ' ἔργμασι πειθόμενοι

.   .   .   .

οὔθ' ἱερῶν κτεάνων οὔτε τι δημοσίων
φειδόμενοι κλέπτουσιν ἐφ' ἁρπαγῇ ἄλλοθεν ἄλλος
οὐδὲ φυλάσσονται σεμνὰ Δίκης θέμεθλα,
ἣ σιγῶσα σύνοιδε τὰ γιγνόμενα πρό τ' ἐόντα,
τῷ δὲ χρόνῳ πάντως ἦλθ' ἀποτεισομένη.   15
τοῦτ' ἤδη πάσῃ πόλει ἔρχεται ἕλκος ἄφυκτον·
ἐς δὲ κακὴν ταχέως ἤλυθε δουλοσύνην,

ἢ στάσιν ἔμφυλον πόλεμόν θ᾽ εὕδοντ᾽ ἐπεγείρει,
  ὃς πολλῶν ἐρατὴν ὤλεσεν ἡλικίην·   20
ἐκ γὰρ δυσμενέων ταχέως πολυήρατον ἄστυ
  τρύχεται ἐν συνόδοις τοῖσ᾽ ἀδικοῦσι φίλαις.
ταῦτα μὲν ἐν δήμῳ στρέφεται κακά· τῶν δὲ πενιχρῶν
  ἱκνοῦνται πολλοὶ γαῖαν ἐς ἀλλοδαπήν
πραθέντες δεσμοῖσί τ᾽ ἀεικελίοισι δεθέντες.   25

. . . .

οὕτω δημόσιον κακὸν ἔρχεται οἴκαδ᾽ ἑκάστῳ·
  αὔλειοι δ᾽ ἔτ᾽ ἔχειν οὐκ ἐθέλουσι θύραι,
ὑψηλὸν δ᾽ ὑπὲρ ἕρκος ὑπέρθορεν, ηὗρε δὲ πάντως,
  εἰ καί τις φεύγων ἐν μυχῷ ᾖ θαλάμου.
ταῦτα διδάξαι θυμὸς Ἀθηναίους με κελεύει,   30
  ὡς κακὰ πλεῖστα πόλει δυσνομίη παρέχει,
εὐνομίη δ᾽ εὔκοσμα καὶ ἄρτια πάντ᾽ ἀποφαίνει
  καὶ θαμὰ τοῖσ᾽ ἀδίκοισ᾽ ἀμφιτίθησι πέδας·
τραχέα λειαίνει, παύει κόρον, ὕβριν ἀμαυροῖ,
  αὐαίνει δ᾽ ἄτης ἄνθεα φυόμενα,   35
εὐθύνει δὲ δίκας σκολιὰς ὑπερήφανά τ᾽ ἔργα
  πραΰνει, παύει δ᾽ ἔργα διχοστασίης,
παύει δ᾽ ἀργαλέης ἔριδος χόλον, ἔστι δ᾽ ὑπ᾽ αὐτῆς
  πάντα κατ᾽ ἀνθρώπους ἄρτια καὶ πινυτά.

4

πολλοὶ γὰρ πλουτοῦσι κακοί, ἀγαθοὶ δὲ πένονται·
  ἀλλ᾽ ἡμεῖς αὐτοῖσ᾽ οὐ διαμειψόμεθα
τῆς ἀρετῆς τὸν πλοῦτον, ἐπεὶ τὸ μὲν ἔμπεδον αἰεί,
  χρήματα δ᾽ ἀνθρώπων ἄλλοτε ἄλλος ἔχει.

5

δήμῳ μὲν γὰρ ἔδωκα τόσον γέρας, ὅσσον ἀπαρκεῖ,
  τιμῆς οὔτ᾽ ἀφελὼν οὔτ᾽ ἐπορεξάμενος·
οἳ δ᾽ εἶχον δύναμιν καὶ χρήμασιν ἦσαν ἀγητοί,
  καὶ τοῖσ᾽ ἐφρασάμην μηδὲν ἀεικὲς ἔχειν·

ἔστην δ᾽ ἀμφιβαλὼν κρατερὸν σάκος ἀμφοτέροισι,   5
   νικᾶν δ᾽ οὐκ εἴασ᾽ οὐδετέρους ἀδίκως.

  .   .   .   .

δῆμος δ᾽ ὧδ᾽ ἂν ἄριστα σὺν ἡγεμόνεσσιν ἔποιτο,
   μήτε λίαν ἀνεθεὶς μήτε βιαζόμενος.
τίκτει γὰρ κόρος ὕβριν, ὅταν πολὺς ὄλβος ἔπηται
   ἀνθρώποισιν ὅσοις μὴ νόος ἄρτιος ᾖ.   10

  .   .   .   .

ἔργμασιν ἐν μεγάλοις πᾶσιν ἀδεῖν χαλεπόν.

10

ἐκ νεφέλης πέλεται χιόνος μένος ἠδὲ χαλάζης,
   βροντὴ δ᾽ ἐκ λαμπρᾶς γίγνεται ἀστεροπῆς·
ἀνδρῶν δ᾽ ἐκ μεγάλων πόλις ὄλλυται· ἐς δὲ μονάρχου
   δῆμος ἀιδρείῃ δουλοσύνην ἔπεσεν·
λίη<ν> δ᾽ ἐξάραντ᾽ οὐ ῥᾴδιόν ἐστι κατασχεῖν   5
   ὕστερον, ἀλλ᾽ ἤδη χρὴ <περὶ> πάντα νοεῖν.

13

Ὄλβιος ᾧ παῖδές τε φίλοι καὶ μώνυχες ἵπποι
   καὶ κύνες ἀγρευταὶ καὶ ξένος ἀλλοδαπός.

21

πολλὰ ψεύδονται ἀοιδοί.

19

Παῖς μὲν ἄνηβος ἐὼν ἔτι νήπιος ἕρκος ὀδόντων
   φύσας ἐκβάλλει πρῶτον ἐν ἔπτ᾽ ἔτεσιν·
τοὺς δ᾽ ἑτέρους ὅτε δὴ τελέσῃ θεὸς ἔπτ᾽ ἐνιαυτούς,
   ἥβης ἐκφαίνει σήματα γιγνομένης·
τῇ τριτάτῃ δὲ γένειον ἀεξομένων ἔτι γυίων   5
   λαχνοῦται, χροιῆς ἄνθος ἀμειβομένης·
τῇ δὲ τετάρτῃ πᾶς τις ἐν ἑβδομάδι μέγ᾽ ἄριστος
   ἰσχύν, ἥντ᾽ ἄνδρες σήματ᾽ ἔχουσ᾽ ἀρετῆς·

πέμπτῃ δ᾽ ὥριον ἄνδρα γάμου μεμνημένον εἶναι
  καὶ παίδων ζητεῖν εἰσοπίσω γενεήν·   15
τῇ δ᾽ ἕκτῃ περὶ πάντα καταρτύεται νόος ἀνδρός
  οὐδ᾽ ἔρδειν ἔθ᾽ ὁμῶς ἔργ᾽ ἀπάλαμνα θέλει·
ἑπτὰ δὲ νοῦν καὶ γλῶσσαν ἐν ἑβδομάσιν μέγ᾽ ἄριστος
  ὀκτώ τ᾽· ἀμφοτέρων τέσσαρα καὶ δέκ᾽ ἔτη·
τῇ δ᾽ ἐνάτῃ ἔτι μὲν δύναται, μαλακώτερα δ᾽ αὐτοῦ   20
  πρὸς μεγάλην ἀρετὴν γλῶσσά τε καὶ σοφίη·
τὴν δεκάτην δ᾽ εἴ τις τελέσας κατὰ μέτρον ἵκοιτο,
  οὐκ ἂν ἄωρος ἐὼν μοῖραν ἔχοι θανάτου.

22

Ἀλλ᾽ εἴ μοι κἂν νῦν ἔτι πείσεαι, ἔξελε τοῦτον,
  μηδὲ μέγαιρ᾽, ὅτι σεῦ λῷον ἐπεφρασάμην,
καὶ μεταποίησον, Λιγυαστάδη, ὧδε δ᾽ ἄειδε·
  ‘ ὀγδωκονταέτη μοῖρα κίχοι θανάτου.’

. . . .

μηδέ μοι ἄκλαυστος θάνατος μόλοι, ἀλλὰ φίλοισι   5
  καλλείποιμι θανὼν ἄλγεα καὶ στοναχάς.

γηράσκω δ᾽ αἰεὶ πολλὰ διδασκόμενος.

XENOPHANES

I

Νῦν γὰρ δὴ ζάπεδον καθαρὸν καὶ χεῖρες ἁπάντων
  καὶ κύλικες· πλεκτοὺς δ᾽ ἀμφιτιθεῖ στεφάνους,
ἄλλος δ᾽ εὐῶδες μύρον ἐν φιάλῃ παρατείνει·
  κρητὴρ δ᾽ ἕστηκεν μεστὸς εὐφροσύνης·
ἄλλος δ᾽ οἶνος ἑτοῖμος, ὃς οὔποτέ φησι προδώσειν,   5
  μείλιχος ἐν κεράμοισ᾽, ἄνθεος ὀζόμενος·
ἐν δὲ μέσοισ᾽ ἁγνὴν ὀδμὴν λιβανωτὸς ἵησι·
  ψυχρὸν δ᾽ ἐστὶν ὕδωρ καὶ γλυκὺ καὶ καθαρόν·

πάρκεινται δ' ἄρτοι ξανθοὶ γεραρή τε τράπεζα
   τυροῦ καὶ μέλιτος πίονος ἀχθομένη·   10
βωμὸς δ' ἄνθεσιν ἂν τὸ μέσον πάντῃ πεπύκασται·
   μολπὴ δ' ἀμφὶς ἔχει δώματα καὶ θαλίη.
χρὴ δὲ πρῶτον μὲν θεὸν ὑμνεῖν εὔφρονας ἄνδρας
   εὐφήμοις μύθοις καὶ καθαροῖσι λόγοις·
σπείσαντας δὲ καὶ εὐξαμένους τὰ δίκαια δύνασθαι   15
   πρήσσειν — ταῦτα γὰρ ὦν ἐστι προχειρότερον —
οὐχ ὕβρις πίνειν ὁπόσον κεν ἔχων ἀφίκοιο
   οἴκαδ' ἄνευ προπόλου μὴ πάνυ γηραλέος·
ἀνδρῶν δ' αἰνεῖν τοῦτον, ὃς ἐσθλὰ πιὼν ἀναφαίνῃ,
   ὥς οἱ μνημοσύνη καὶ τόνος ἀμφ' ἀρετῆς.   20
οὔτι μάχας διέπειν Τιτήνων οὐδὲ Γιγάντων
   οὐδέ τι Κενταύρων, πλάσματα τῶν προτέρων,
ἢ στάσιας σφεδανάς — τοῖσ' οὐδὲν χρηστὸν ἔνεστι —
   θεῶν δὲ προμηθείην αἰὲν ἔχειν ἀγαθόν.

2

Ἀλλ' εἰ μὲν ταχυτῆτι ποδῶν νίκην τις ἄροιτο
   ἢ πενταθλεύων, ἔνθα Διὸς τέμενος
πὰρ Πίσαο ῥοῇσ' ἐν Ὀλυμπίῃ, εἴτε παλαίων
   ἢ καὶ πυκτοσύνην ἀλγινόεσσαν ἔχων,
εἴτε τὸ δεινὸν ἄεθλον, ὃ παγκράτιον καλέουσιν,   5
   ἀστοῖσίν κ' εἴη κυδρότερος προσορᾶν
καί κε προεδρίην φανερὴν ἀγῶσιν ἄροιτο
   καί κεν σῖτ' εἴη δημοσίων κτεάνων
ἐκ πόλιος καὶ δῶρον, ὅ οἱ κειμήλιον εἴη·
   εἴτε καὶ ἵπποισιν, ταῦτά κε πάντα λάχοι,   10
οὐκ ἐὼν ἄξιος ὥσπερ ἐγώ· ῥώμης γὰρ ἀμείνων
   ἀνδρῶν ἠδ' ἵππων ἡμετέρη σοφίη.
ἀλλ' εἰκῆ μάλα τοῦτο νομίζεται, οὐδὲ δίκαιον
   προκρίνειν ῥώμην τῆς ἀγαθῆς σοφίης.
οὔτε γὰρ εἰ πύκτης ἀγαθὸς λαοῖσι μετείη   15
   οὔτ' εἰ πενταθλεῖν οὔτε παλαισμοσύνην,
οὐδὲ μὲν εἰ ταχυτῆτι ποδῶν, τόπερ ἐστὶ πρότιμον,

ῥώμης ὅσσ᾽ ἀνδρῶν ἔργ᾽ ἐν ἀγῶνι πέλει,
τοὔνεκεν ἂν δὴ μᾶλλον ἐν εὐνομίῃ πόλις εἴη·
σμικρὸν δ᾽ ἄν τι πόλει χάρμα γένοιτ᾽ ἐπὶ τῷ,
εἴ τις ἀεθλεύων νικῷ Πίσαο παρ᾽ ὄχθας·
οὐ γὰρ πιαίνει ταῦτα μυχοὺς πόλιος.

20

10

Πάντα θεοῖσ᾽ ἀνέθηκαν Ὅμηρός θ᾽ Ἡσίοδός τε,
ὅσσα παρ᾽ ἀνθρώποισιν ὀνείδεα καὶ ψόγος ἐστίν,
κλέπτειν μοιχεύειν τε καὶ ἀλλήλους ἀπατεύειν.

12

ἀλλ᾽ οἱ βροτοὶ δοκέουσι γεννᾶσθαι θεούς,
τὴν σφετέρην δ᾽ ἐσθῆτα ἔχειν φωνήν τε δέμας τε.

13

ἀλλ᾽ εἰ χεῖρας ἔχον γε βόες θ᾽ ἵπποι τ᾽, ἐθέλοντες
ἢ γράψαι χείρεσσιν ἢ ἔργα τελεῖν ἅπερ ἄνδρες,
ἵπποι μέν θ᾽ ἵπποισι, βόες δέ τε βουσὶν ὁμοίας
καί κε θεῶν ἰδέας ἔγραφον, καὶ σώματ᾽ ἐποίουν
τοιαῦθ᾽, οἷόν περ καὐτοὶ δέμας εἶχον ἕκαστοι.

14

Αἰθίοπές τε θεοὺς σφετέρους σιμοὺς μέλανάς τε
Θρῆκές τε γλαυκοὺς καὶ πυρρούς φασι πέλεσθαι.

16

οὔτοι ἀπ᾽ ἀρχῆς πάντα θεοὶ θνητοῖσ᾽ ὑπέδειξαν,
ἀλλὰ χρόνῳ ζητοῦντες ἐφευρίσκουσιν ἄμεινον.

18

Πὰρ πυρὶ χρὴ τοιαῦτα λέγειν χειμῶνος ἐν ὥρῃ
ἐν κλίνῃ μαλακῇ κατακείμενον, ἔμπλεον ὄντα,
πίνοντα γλυκὺν οἶνον, ὑποτρώγοντ᾽ ἐρεβίνθους·
῾ τίς πόθεν εἰς ἀνδρῶν; πόσα τοι ἔτε᾽ ἐστί, φέριστε;
πηλίκος ἦσθ᾽ ὅθ᾽ ὁ Μῆδος ἀφίκετο; ᾽

5

19

Εἷς θεὸς ἔν τε θεοῖσι καὶ ἀνθρώποισι μέγιστος,
οὔτι δέμας θνητοῖσιν ὁμοίιος οὐδὲ νόημα.

20

οὖλος ὁρᾷ, οὖλος δὲ νοεῖ, οὖλος δέ τ᾽ ἀκούει.

23

ἐκ γαίης γὰρ πάντα καὶ εἰς γῆν πάντα τελευτᾷ.

28

ἥν τ᾽ Ἶριν καλέουσι, νέφος καὶ τοῦτο πέφυκε,
πορφύρεον καὶ φοινίκεον καὶ χλωρὸν ἰδέσθαι.

29

πάντες γὰρ γαίης τε καὶ ὕδατος ἐκγενόμεσθα.

30

καὶ τὸ μὲν οὖν σαφὲς οὔτις ἀνὴρ γένετ᾽ οὐδέ τις ἔσται,
εἰδὼς ἀμφὶ θεῶν τε καὶ ἅσσα λέγω περὶ πάντων·
εἰ γὰρ καὶ τὰ μάλιστα τύχοι τετελεσμένον εἰπών,
αὐτὸς ὅμως οὐκ οἶδε· δόκος δ᾽ ἐπὶ πᾶσι τέτυκται.

THEOGNIS

Σοὶ δ᾽ ἐγὼ εὖ φρονέων ὑποθήσομαι, οἷά περ αὐτός,
   Κύρν᾽, ἀπὸ τῶν ἀγαθῶν παῖς ἔτ᾽ ἐὼν ἔμαθον.
πέπνυσο μηδ᾽ αἰσχροῖσιν ἐπ᾽ ἔργμασι μηδ᾽ ἀδίκοισιν
   τιμὰς μηδ᾽ ἀρετὰς ἕλκεο μηδ᾽ ἄφενος.   30
ταῦτα μὲν οὕτως ἴσθι· κακοῖσι δὲ μὴ προσομίλει
   ἀνδράσιν, ἀλλ᾽ αἰεὶ τῶν ἀγαθῶν ἔχεο.

Κύρνε, πόλις μὲν ἔθ᾽ ἥδε πόλις, λαοὶ δὲ δὴ ἄλλοι·
   οἳ πρόσθ᾽ οὔτε δίκας ᾔδεσαν οὔτε νόμους,

ἀλλ' ἀμφὶ πλευρῆσι δορὰς αἰγῶν κατέτριβον,   55
ἔξω δ' ὥστ' ἔλαφοι τῆσδ' ἐνέμοντο πόλεος,
καὶ νῦν εἰσ' ἀγαθοί, Πολυπαΐδη· οἱ δὲ πρὶν ἐσθλοί
νῦν δειλοί. τίς κεν ταῦτ' ἀνέχοιτ' ἐσορῶν;

. . . .

Μήποτε, Κύρνε, κακῷ πίσυνος βούλευε σὺν ἀνδρί,
εὖτ' ἂν σπουδαῖον πρῆγμ' ἐθέλῃς τελέσαι,   70
ἀλλὰ μετ' ἐσθλὸν ἰὼν βουλεύεο πολλὰ μογήσας
καὶ μακρὴν ποσσίν, Κύρν', ὁδὸν ἐκτελέσας.

. . . .

Πιστὸς ἀνὴρ χρυσοῦ τε καὶ ἀργύρου ἀντερύσασθαι   77
ἄξιος ἐν καλεπῇ, Κύρνε, διχοστασίῃ.

. . . .

Μή μ' ἔπεσιν μὲν στέργε, νόον δ' ἔχε καὶ φρένας ἄλλῃ,
εἴ με φιλεῖς καί τοι πιστὸς ἔνεστι νόος.
Ἢ με φίλει καθαρὸν θέμενος νόον ἤ μ' ἀποειπών
ἔχθαιρ' ἀμφαδίην νεῖκος ἀειράμενος.   90
ὃς δὲ μιῇ γλώσσῃ δίχ' ἔχει νόον, οὗτος ἑταῖρος
δεινός, Κύρν', ἐχθρὸς βέλτερος ἢ φίλος ὤν.

. . . .

Ἄνδρ' ἀγαθὸν πενίη πάντων δάμνησι μάλιστα,
καὶ γήρως πολιοῦ, Κύρνε, καὶ ἠπιάλου.
Χρὴ πενίην φεύγοντα καὶ ἐς βαθυκήτεα πόντον
ῥιπτεῖν καὶ πετρέων, Κύρνε, κατ' ἠλιβάτων.   175
Πᾶς γὰρ ἀνὴρ πενίῃ δεδμημένος οὔτε τι εἰπεῖν
οὔθ' ἔρξαι δύναται, γλῶσσα δέ οἱ δέδεται.

. . . .

Κριοὺς μὲν καὶ ὄνους διζήμεθα, Κύρνε, καὶ ἵππους
εὐγενέας, καί τις βούλεται ἐξ ἀγαθῶν
κτήσασθαι· γῆμαι δὲ κακὴν κακοῦ οὐ μελεδαίνει   185
ἐσθλὸς ἀνήρ, ἤν οἱ χρήματα πολλὰ διδῷ,
οὐδὲ γυνὴ κακοῦ ἀνδρὸς ἀναίνεται εἶναι ἄκοιτις
πλουσίου, ἀλλ' ἀφνεὸν βούλεται ἀντ' ἀγαθοῦ.

χρήματα γὰρ τιμῶσι· καὶ ἐκ κακοῦ ἐσθλὸς ἔγημε
   καὶ κακὸς ἐξ ἀγαθοῦ· πλοῦτος ἔμειξε γένος.   190
οὕτω μὴ θαύμαζε γένος, Πολυπαΐδη, ἀστῶν
   μαυροῦσθαι· σὺν γὰρ μίσγεται ἐσθλὰ κακοῖς.

. . . .

Οὐδείς τοι φεύγοντι φίλος καὶ πιστὸς ἑταῖρος·
   τῆς δὲ φυγῆς ἐστιν τοῦτ' ἀνιηρότερον.   210

. . . .

Κύρνε, φίλους κατὰ πάντας ἐπίστρεφε ποικίλον ἦθος,
   ὀργὴν συμμίσγων ἥντιν' ἕκαστος ἔχει·
πουλύπου ὀργὴν ἴσχε πολυπλόκου, ὃς ποτὶ πέτρη,   215
   τῇ προσομιλήσῃ, τοῖος ἰδεῖν ἐφάνη.
νῦν μὲν τῇδ' ἐφέπου, τοτὲ δ' ἀλλοῖς χρόα γίνου.
   κρέσσων τοι σοφίη γίνεται ἀτροπίης.

. . . .

Εὖ κώτιλλε τὸν ἐχθρόν· ὅταν δ' ὑποχείριος ἔλθῃ,   363
   τεῖσαί μιν πρόφασιν μηδεμίαν θέμενος.

. . . .

Ἐν πενίῃ δ' ὅ τε δειλὸς ἀνὴρ ὅ τε πολλὸν ἀμείνων
   φαίνεται, εὖτ' ἂν δὴ χρημοσύνη κατέχῃ·
τοῦ μὲν γὰρ τὰ δίκαια φρονεῖ νόος, οὗ τέ περ αἰεί   395
   ἰθεῖα γνώμη στήθεσιν ἐμπεφύῃ·
τοῦ δ' αὖτ' οὔτε κακοῖσ' ἕπεται νόος οὔτ' ἀγαθοῖσιν.
   τὸν δ' ἀγαθὸν τολμᾶν χρὴ τά τε καὶ τὰ φέρειν.

. . . .

Ὤ μοι ἐγὼν ἥβης καὶ γήραος οὐλομένοιο,   527
   τοῦ μὲν ἐπερχομένου, τῆς δ' ἀπονισσομένης.

. . . .

Αἰεί μοι φίλον ἦτορ ἰαίνεται, ὁππότ' ἀκούσω   531
   αὐλῶν φθεγγομένων ἱμερόεσσαν ὄπα.

. . . .

Χαίρω δ᾽ εὖ πίνων καὶ ὑπ᾽ αὐλητῆρος ἀείδων,   533
  χαίρω δ᾽ εὔφθογγον χερσὶ λύρην ὀχέων.

.   .   .   .

Οἵ με φίλοι προδιδοῦσιν, ἐπεὶ τόν γ᾽ ἐχθρὸν ἀλεῦμαι   575
  ὥστε κυβερνήτης χοιράδας εἰναλίας.

.   .   .   .

Πολλῷ τοι πλέονας λιμοῦ κόρος ὤλεσεν ἤδη   605
  ἄνδρας, ὅσοι μοίρης πλεῖον ἔχειν ἔθελον.

.   .   .   .

Λὰξ ἐπίβα δήμῳ κενεόφρονι, τύπτε δὲ κέντρῳ
  ὀξέι καὶ ζεύγλην δύσλοφον ἀμφιτίθει·
οὐ γὰρ ἔθ᾽ εὑρήσεις δῆμον φιλοδέσποτον ὧδε,
  ἀνθρώπων ὁπόσους ἠέλιος καθορᾷ.   850

Ἡμεῖς δ᾽ ἐν θαλίῃσι φίλον καταθώμεθα θυμόν,
  ὄφρ᾽ ἔτι τερπωλῆς ἔργ᾽ ἐρατεινὰ φέρῃ.
αἶψα γὰρ ὥστε νόημα παρέρχεται ἀγλαὸς ἥβη·   985
  οὐ δ᾽ ἵππων ὁρμὴ γίνεται ὠκυτέρη,
αἵτε ἄνακτα φέρουσι δορυσσόον ἐς πόνον ἀνδρῶν
  λάβρως πυροφόρῳ τερπόμεναι πεδίῳ.

Ὄρνιθος φωνήν, Πολυπαΐδη, ὀξὺ βοώσης
  ἤκουσ᾽, ἥτε βροτοῖσ᾽ ἄγγελος ἦλθ᾽ ἀρότου
ὡραίου· καί μοι κραδίην ἐπάταξε μέλαιναν,
  ὅττι μοι εὐανθέας ἄλλοι ἔχουσιν ἀγρούς.   1200

.   .   .   .

Σοὶ μὲν ἐγὼ πτέρ᾽ ἔδωκα σὺν οἷσ᾽ ἐπ᾽ ἀπείρονα πόντον
  πωτήσει καὶ γῆν πᾶσαν ἀειρόμενος
ῥηϊδίως· θοίνῃς δὲ καὶ εἰλαπίνῃσι παρέσσῃ
  ἐν πάσαις πολλῶν κείμενος ἐν στόμασιν,   240
καί σε σὺν αὐλίσκοισι λιγυφθόγγοις νέοι ἄνδρες
  εὐκόσμως ἐρατοὶ καλά τε καὶ λιγέα
ᾄσονται. καὶ ὅταν δνοφερῆς ὑπὸ κεύθεσι γαίης

βῆς πολυκωκύτους εἰς Ἀίδαο δόμους,
οὐδέποτ᾽ οὐδὲ θανὼν ἀπολεῖς κλέος, ἀλλὰ μελήσεις   245
    ἄφθιτον ἀνθρώποισ᾽ αἰὲν ἔχων ὄνομα,
Κύρνε, καθ᾽ Ἑλλάδα γῆν στρωφώμενος ἠδ᾽ ἀνὰ νήσους
    ἰχθυόεντα περῶν πόντον ἐπ᾽ ἀτρύγετον,
οὐχ ἵππων νώτοισιν ἐφήμενος· ἀλλά σε πέμψει
    ἀγλαὰ Μουσάων δῶρα ἰοστεφάνων.   250
πᾶσι δ᾽, ὅσοισι μέμηλε, καὶ ἐσσομένοισιν ἀοιδή
    ἔσσῃ ὁμῶς, ὄφρ᾽ ἂν γῆ τε καὶ ἠέλιος.
αὐτὰρ ἐγὼν ὀλίγης παρὰ σεῦ οὐ τυγχάνω αἰδοῦς,
    ἀλλ᾽ ὥσπερ μικρὸν παῖδα λόγοις μ᾽ ἀπατᾷς.

ARCHILOCHUS

1

Εἰμὶ δ᾽ ἐγὼ θεράπων μὲν Ἐνυαλίοιο ἄνακτος
    καὶ Μουσέων ἐρατὸν δῶρον ἐπιστάμενος.

2

Ἐν δορὶ μέν μοι μᾶζα μεμαγμένη, ἐν δορὶ δ᾽ οἶνος
    Ἰσμαρικός, πίνω δ᾽ ἐν δορὶ κεκλιμένος.

3

Οὔ τοι πόλλ᾽ ἐπὶ τόξα τανύσσεται οὐδὲ θαμειαί
σφενδόναι, εὖτ᾽ ἂν δὴ μῶλον Ἄρης συνάγῃ
ἐν πεδίῳ· ξιφέων δὲ πολύστονον ἔσσεται ἔργον·
ταύτης γὰρ κεῖνοι αἵμονές εἰσι μάχης
δεσπόται Εὐβοίης δουρικλυτοί.

6

Ἀσπίδι μὲν Σαΐων τις ἀγάλλεται, ἣν παρὰ θάμνῳ
ἔντος ἀμώμητον κάλλιπον οὐκ ἐθέλων·
αὐτὸς δ᾽ ἐξέφυγον θανάτου τέλος· ἀσπὶς ἐκείνη
ἐρρέτω· ἐξαῦτις κτήσομαι οὐ κακίω.

7

Κήδεα μὲν στονόεντα, Περίκλεες, οὔτε τις ἀστῶν
    μεμφόμενος θαλίης τέρψεται οὐδὲ πόλις·
τοίους γὰρ κατὰ κῦμα πολυφλοίσβοιο θαλάσσης
    ἔκλυσεν· οἰδαλέους δ᾽ ἀμφ᾽ ὀδύνῃσ᾽ ἔχομεν
πνεύμονας. ἀλλὰ θεοὶ γὰρ ἀνηκέστοισι κακοῖσιν,   5
    ὦ φίλ᾽, ἐπὶ κρατερὴν τλημοσύνην ἔθεσαν
φάρμακον. ἄλλοτέ τ᾽ ἄλλος ἔχει τάδε· νῦν μὲν ἐς ἡμέας
    ἐτράπεθ᾽, αἱματόεν δ᾽ ἕλκος ἀναστένομεν,
ἐξαῦτις δ᾽ ἑτέρους ἐπαμείψεται. ἀλλὰ τάχιστα
    τλῆτε γυναικεῖον πένθος ἀπωσάμενοι.   10

18

    ἥδε δ᾽ ὥστ᾽ ὄνου ῥάχις
ἔστηκεν ὕλης ἀγρίης ἐπιστεφής.

 .   .   .   .

οὐ γάρ τι καλὸς χῶρος οὐδ᾽ ἐφίμερος
οὐδ᾽ ἐρατός, οἷος ἀμφι Σίριος ῥοάς.

22

Οὔ μοι τὰ Γύγεω τοῦ πολυχρύσου μέλει
οὐδ᾽ εἷλέ πώ με ζῆλος οὐδ᾽ ἀγαίομαι
θεῶν ἔργα, μεγάλης δ᾽ οὐκ ἐρέω τυραννίδος·
ἀπόπροθεν γάρ ἐστιν ὀφθαλμῶν ἐμῶν.

25

ἔχουσα θαλλὸν μυρσίνης ἐτέρπετο
ῥοδῆς τε καλὸν ἄνθος,
                    ἡ δέ οἱ κόμη
ὤμους κατεσκίαζε καὶ μετάφρενα.

53

ἔα Πάρον καὶ σῦκα κεῖνα καὶ θαλάσσιον βίον.

54

ὡς Πανελλήνων ὀιζὺς ἐς Θάσον συνέδραμεν.

58

Τοῖς θεοῖς τίθει ἅπαντα· πολλάκις μὲν ἐκ κακῶν
ἄνδρας ὀρθοῦσιν μελαίνῃ κειμένους ἐπὶ χθονί,
πολλάκις δ᾽ ἀνατρέπουσι καὶ μάλ᾽ εὖ βεβηκότας
ὑπτίους κλίνουσ᾽· ἔπειτα πολλὰ γίγνεται κακά,
καὶ βίου χρήμῃ πλανᾶται καὶ νόου παρήορος.

60

Οὐ φιλέω μέγαν στρατηγὸν οὐδὲ διαπεπλιγμένον
οὐδὲ βοστρύχοισι γαῦρον οὐδ᾽ ὑπεξυρημένον·
ἀλλά μοι σμικρός τις εἴη καὶ περὶ κνήμας ἰδεῖν
ῥοικός, ἀσφαλέως βεβηκὼς ποσσί, καρδίης πλέως.

66

ἓν δ᾽ ἐπίσταμαι μέγα,
τὸν κακῶς με δρῶντα δεινοῖσ᾽ ἀνταμείβεσθαι κακοῖς.

67

Θυμέ, θύμ᾽ ἀμηχάνοισι κήδεσιν κυκώμενε,
ἀνάδυ, δυσμενῶν δ᾽ ἀλέξευ προσβαλὼν ἐναντίον
στέρνον, ἐν λόχοισι δ᾽ ἐχθρῶν πλησίον κατασταθεὶς
ἀσφαλέως· καὶ μήτε νικῶν ἀμφάδην ἀγάλλεο
μηδὲ νικηθεὶς ἐν οἴκῳ καταπεσὼν ὀδύρεο·
ἀλλὰ χαρτοῖσίν τε χαῖρε καὶ κακοῖσιν ἀσχάλα
μὴ λίην· γίγνωσκε δ᾽ οἷος ῥυσμὸς ἀνθρώπους ἔχει.

5

71

εἰ γὰρ ὣς ἐμοὶ γένοιτο χεῖρα Νεοβούλης θιγεῖν.

74

Χρημάτων ἄελπτον οὐδέν ἐστιν οὐδ᾽ ἀπώμοτον
οὐδὲ θαυμάσιον, ἐπειδὴ Ζεὺς πατὴρ Ὀλυμπίων

ἐκ μεσημβρίης ἔθηκε νύκτ᾽ ἀποκρύψας φάος
ἡλίου λάμποντος· λυγρὸν δ᾽ ἦλθ᾽ ἐπ᾽ ἀνθρώπους δέος.
ἐκ δὲ τοῦ καὶ πιστὰ πάντα κἀπίελπτα γίγνεται   5
ἀνδράσιν· μηδεὶς ἔθ᾽ ὑμέων εἰσορῶν θαυμαζέτω,
μηδ᾽ ὅταν δελφῖσι θῆρες ἀνταμείψωνται νομόν
ἐνάλιον καί σφιν θαλάσσης ἠχέεντα κύματα
φίλτερ᾽ ἠπείρου γένηται, τοῖσι δ᾽ ἡδὺ ᾖ ὄρος.

77

ὡς Διωνύσοι᾽ ἄνακτος καλὸν ἐξάρξαι μέλος
οἶδα διθύραμβον οἴνῳ συγκεραυνωθεὶς φρένας.

88

Πάτερ Λυκάμβα, ποῖον ἐφράσω τόδε;
    τίς σὰς παρήειρε φρένας,
ᾗς τὸ πρὶν ἠρήρεισθα; νῦν δὲ δὴ πολύς
    ἀστοῖσι φαίνεαι γέλως.

89

    Αἶνός τις ἀνθρώπων ὅδε,
ὡς ἆρ᾽ ἀλώπηξ καἰετὸς ξυνωνίην
    ἔμειξαν.

90

προύθηκε παισὶ δεῖπνον αἰηνὲς φέρων.

92

'Ὁρᾷς ἵν᾽ ἔστ᾽ ἐκεῖνος ὑψηλὸς πάγος
    τρηχύς τε καὶ παλίγκοτος;
ἐν τῷ κάθημαι σὴν ἐλαφρίζων μάχην.

. . . .

    λαιψηρὰ κυκλῶσαι πτερά
ἐκ γῆς τ᾽ ἀνίπτασθαι πρὸς ὑψηλὸν πάγον   5
    ἀρθεῖσαν οὕτως . . .'

94

' Ὦ Ζεῦ πάτερ Ζεῦ, σὸν μὲν οὐρανοῦ κράτος,
σὺ δ' ἔργ' ἐπ' ἀνθρώπων ὁρᾷς
λεωργὰ καὶ θεμιστά, σοὶ δὲ θηρίων
ὕβρις τε καὶ δίκη μέλει.'

HIPPONAX

Δύ' ἡμέραι γυναικός εἰσιν ἥδισται,
ὅταν γαμῇ τις κἀκφέρῃ τεθνηκυῖαν.

ALCMAN

58

Εὕδουσιν δ' ὀρέων κορυφαί τε καὶ φάραγγες,
πρώονές τε καὶ χαράδραι,
φῦλά τ' ἑρπετὰ τόσσα τρέφει μέλαινα γαῖα,
θῆρές τ' ὀρεσκῷοι καὶ γένος μελισσᾶν
καὶ κνώδαλ' ἐν βένθεσσι πορφυρέας ἁλός·   5
εὕδουσιν δ' οἰωνῶν
φῦλα τανυπτερύγων.

94

Οὔ μ' ἔτι, παρθενικαὶ μελιγάρυες ἱμερόφωνοι,
γυῖα φέρειν δύναται· βάλε δή, βάλε κηρύλος εἴην,
ὅστ' ἐπὶ κύματος ἄνθος ἅμ' ἀλκυόνεσσι ποτῆται
νηδεὲς ἦτορ ἔχων, ἁλιπόρφυρος ἱαρὸς ὄρνις.

STESICHORUS

6

Ἀέλιος δ' Ὑπεριονίδας δέπας ἐσκατέβαινε
χρύσεον, ὄφρα δι' Ὠκεανοῖο περάσας
ἀφίκοιθ ἱερᾶς ποτὶ βένθεα νυκτὸς ἐρεμνᾶς

ποτὶ ματέρα κουριδίαν τ᾽ ἄλοχον παῖδάς τε φίλους·
ὁ δ᾽ ἐς ἄλσος ἔβα   5
δάφναισι κατάσκιον ποσσὶ πάϊς Διός.

10

πολλὰ μὲν Κυδώνια μᾶλα ποτερρίπτευν ποτὶ δίφρον ἄνακτι,
πολλὰ δὲ μύρσινα φύλλα
καὶ ῥοδίνους στεφάνους ἴων τε κορωνίδας οὔλας.

ALCAEUS

2

Χαῖρε, Κυλλάνας ὁ μέδεις, σὲ γάρ μοι
θῦμος ὕμνην, τὸν κορύφαισιν ἄγνα
Μαῖα γέννατο Κρονίδα μίγεισα
            παμβασίληϊ.

30

Ἀσυννέτημι τῶν ἀνέμων στάσιν·
τὸ μὲν γὰρ ἔνθεν κῦμα κυλίνδεται,
    τὸ δ᾽ ἔνθεν· ἄμμες δ᾽ ὂν τὸ μέσσον
        νᾶϊ φορήμεθα σὺν μελαίνᾳ,
χείμωνι μόχθεντες μεγάλῳ μάλα·   5
πὲρ μὲν γὰρ ἄντλος ἰστοπέδαν ἔχει,
    λαῖφος δὲ πὰν ζάδηλον ἤδη
        καὶ λάκιδες μέγαλαι κατ᾽ αὖτο·
χόλαισι δ᾽ ἄγκυραι.

39

Νῦν χρὴ μεθύσθην καί τινα πὲρ βίαν
πώνην, ἐπειδὴ κάτθανε Μύρσιλος.

90

Ὕει μὲν ὁ Ζεῦς, ἐκ δ᾽ ὀράνω μέγας
χείμων, πεπάγαισιν δ᾽ ὑδάτων ῥόαι.

. . . .

κάββαλλε τὸν χείμων᾽ ἐπὶ μὲν τίθεις
πῦρ, ἐν δὲ κέρναις οἶνον ἀφειδέως
　　μέλιχρον, αὖταρ ἀμφὶ κόρσᾳ　　　　　5
　　　μάλθακον ἀμφιβάλων γνόφαλλον.

91

Οὐ χρὴ κάκοισι θῦμον ἐπιτρέπην·
προκόψομεν γὰρ οὐδὲν ἀσάμενοι,
　　ὦ Βύκχι. φάρμακον δ᾽ ἄριστον
　　　οἶνον ἐνεικαμένοις μεθύσθην.

50

Ἦλθες ἐκ περάτων γᾶς ἐλεφαντίναν
λάβαν τῶ ξίφεος χρυσοδέταν ἔχων. . . .
συμμάχεις δ᾽ ἐτέλεσσας Βαβυλωνίοισ᾽
ἄεθλον μέγαν, ἐρρύσαο δ᾽ ἐκ πόνων,
κτένναις ἄνδρα μαχαίταν βασιληίων
παλάσταν ἀπυλείποντα μόναν ἴαν
παχέων ἀπὺ πέμπων. . . .

63

Ἰόπλοκ᾽ ἄγνα μελλιχόμειδε Σάπφοι

66

Οἶνος, ὦ φίλε παῖ, καὶ ἀλάθεα

98

Ἦρος ἀνθεμόεντος ἐπάιον ἐρχομένοιο.
. . . .
ἐν δὲ κέρνατε τῶ μελιάδεος ὄττι τάχιστα
κράτηρα.

104

οἶνος γὰρ ἀνθρώποισι δίοπτρον.

97

Μηδὲν ἄλλο φυτεύσῃς πρότερον δένδριον ἀμπέλω.

54

Μαρμαίρει δὲ μέγας δόμος χάλκῳ· παῖσα δ᾽ ῎Αρῃ κεκόσμη-
    ται στέγα
λάμπραισιν κυνίαισι, κὰτ τᾶν λεῦκοι κατύπερθεν ἴππιοι
    λόφοι
νεύοισιν, κεφάλαισιν ἄνδρων ἀγάλματα· χάλκιαι δὲ
    πασσάλοις
κρύπτοισιν περικείμεναι λάμπραι κνάμιδες, ἄρκος ἰσχύρω
    βέλευς,
θώρακές τε νέω λίνω κοίλαί τε κατ᾽ ἄσπιδες βεβλήμεναι·   5
πὰρ δὲ Χαλκίδικαι σπάθαι, πὰρ δὲ ζώμματα πόλλα καὶ
    κυπάσσιδες·
τῶν οὐκ ἔστι λάθεσθ᾽, ἐπειδὴ πρώτιστ᾽ ὑπὰ ϝέργον ἔσταμεν
    τόδε.

SAPPHO

I

Ποικιλόθρον᾽ ἀθάνατ᾽ ᾽Αφρόδιτα,
παῖ Δίος δολόπλοκε, λίσσομαί σε,
μή μ᾽ ἄσαισι μηδ᾽ ὀνίαισι δάμνα,
    πότνια, θῦμον,
ἀλλὰ τυῖδ᾽ ἔλθ᾽, αἴ ποτα κἀτέρωτα   5
τᾶς ἔμας αὔδως ἀίοισα πήλυι
ἔκλυες, πάτρος δὲ δόμον λίποισα
    χρύσιον ἦλθες
ἄρμ᾽ ὑπασδεύξαισα· κάλοι δέ σ᾽ ἆγον
ὤκεες στροῦθοι περὶ γᾶς μελαίνας   10
πύκνα δίννηντες πτέρ᾽ ἀπ᾽ ὀρράνω αἴθε-
    ρος διὰ μέσσω.

αἶψα δ' ἐξίκοντο, σὺ δ', ὦ μάκαιρα,
μειδιάσαισ' ἀθανάτῳ προσώπῳ
ἤρε', ὅττι δηὖτε πέπονθα κὤττι   15
    δηὖτε κάλημμι
κὤττι μοι μάλιστα θέλω γένεσθαι
μαινόλᾳ θύμῳ. ᾽τίνα δηὖτε Πείθω
μαῖσ' ἄγην εἰς σὰν φιλότατα, τίς σ', ὦ
    Ψάπφ', ἀδικήει;   20
καὶ γὰρ αἰ φεύγει, ταχέως διώξει,
αἰ δὲ δῶρα μὴ δέκετ', ἀλλὰ δώσει,
αἰ δὲ μὴ φίλει, ταχέως φιλήσει
    κωὐκ ἐθέλοισα.᾽
ἔλθε μοι καὶ νῦν, χαλέπαν δὲ λῦσον   25
ἐκ μερίμναν, ὅσσα δέ μοι τέλεσσαι
θῦμος ἰμέρρει, τέλεσον, σὺ δ' αὔτα
    σύμμαχος ἔσσο.

2

Φαίνεταί μοι κῆνος ἴσος θέοισιν
ἔμμεν' ὤνηρ, ὅττις ἐνάντιός τοι
ἰσδάνει καὶ πλάσιον ἆδυ φωνεί-
    σας ὑπακούει
καὶ γελαίσας ἰμέροεν, τό μ' ἦ μάν   5
καρδίαν ἐν στήθεσιν ἐπτόησεν.
ὡς γὰρ εἰσίδω βροχέως σε, φώνας
    οὐδὲν ἔτ' ἴκει,
ἀλλὰ κὰμ μὲν γλῶσσα ϝέαγε, λέπτον δ'
αὔτικα χρῷ πῦρ ὑπαδεδρόμηκεν,   10
ὀππάτεσσι δ' οὐδὲν ὄρημμ', ἐπιρρόμ-
    βεισι δ' ἄκουαι,
κὰδ δέ μ' ἴδρως κακχέεται, τρόμος δέ
παῖσαν ἄγρει, χλωροτέρα δὲ ποίας
ἔμμι, τεθνάκην δ' ὀλίγω 'πιδεύης   15
    φαίνομ', Ἄγαλλι.
ἀλλὰ πᾶν τόλματον, ἐπεί κεν ᾖ τά.

4

Ἄστερες μὲν ἀμφὶ κάλαν σελάνναν
ἂψ ἀπυκρύπτοισι φάεννον εἶδος,
ὄπποτα πλήθοισα μάλιστα λάμπῃ
γᾶν ἐπὶ παῖσαν . . .

5

χάριεν μὲν ἄλσος
μαλίαν, βῶμοι δ' ἔνι θυμιάμε-
νοι λιβανώτῳ,
ἐν δ' ὕδωρ ψῦχρον κελάδει δι' ὔσδων
μαλίνων, ϝρόδοισι δὲ παῖς ὁ χῶρος   10
ἐσκίαστ', αἰθυσσομένων δὲ φύλλων
κῶμα κατέρρει.
ἐν δὲ λείμων ἱππόβοτος τέθαλεν
ἠρίνοισιν ἄνθεσιν, αἰ δ' ἄνητοι
μέλλιχα πνέοισιν ◡ — ◡ — ◡   15
— ◡ ◡ — ◡

ἔλθε δὴ σύ — ◡ ◡ — ◡ Κύπρι,
χρυσίαισιν ἐν κυλίκεσσιν ἄβρως
ἐμμεμείχμενον θαλίαισι νέκταρ
οἰνοχόεισα.   20

27a

Οἰ μὲν ἰππήων στρότον, οἰ δὲ πέσδων,
οἰ δὲ νάων φαῖσ' ἐπί γᾶν μέλαιναν
ἔμμεναι κάλλιστον, ἔγω δὲ κῆν' ὄττω τις ἔραται.
πάγχυ δ' εὔμαρες σύνετον πόησαι   5
πάντι τοῦτ'· ἀ γὰρ πόλυ περσκέθοισα
[κάλλος ἀνθ]ρώπων Ἐλένα τὸν ἄνδρα
[πρῶλιπ' ἄρ]ιστον,
[ὡς τὸ πρὶν] σέβας Τροΐας ὄλεσθαι,
[κωὔδε π]αῖδος οὐδὲ φίλων τοκήων   10

[οὐδὲν] ἐμνάσθη, ἀλλὰ παράγαγ' αὖταν
    [αὔτικ' ἴδοι]σαν
[Κύπρις· εὔγν]αμπτον γὰρ [ἔχοισι νύμφαι]
[καρδίαν], κούφως τ[ε Πόθος πτ]όησιν
[ὅς] με νῦν 'Ανακτορίας ὀνέμναι-   15
    [σ' οὐ] παρεοίσας,
[τᾶ]ς κε βολλοίμαν ἔρατόν τε βᾶμα
κἀμάρυγμα λάμπρον ἴδην προσώπω,
ἢ τὰ Λύδων ἄρματα κἀν ὅπλοισι
    [πεσδομ]άχεντας.   20

40

'Ηράμαν μὲν ἔγω σέθεν, "Ατθι, πάλαι ποτά.

41

σμίκρα μοι πάις ἔμμεν ἐφαίνεο κἄχαρις.

50

    ἐτίναξεν ἔμας φρένας
"Ερος ὡς ἄνεμος κατ' ὄρος δρύσιν ἐμπέσων.

51

ὡς δὲ παῖς πεδὰ μάτερα πεπτερύγωμαι

55a

' "Εκτωρ καὶ συνέταιροι ἄγοισ' ἐλικώπιδα   5
Θήβας ἐξ ἱέρας Πλακίας τ' ἀπ' ἀϊννάω
ἄβραν 'Ανδρομάχαν ἐνὶ ναῦσιν ἐπ' ἄλμυρον
πόντον· πόλλα δ' ἐλίγματα χρύσια κἄμματα
πορφύρα κάλα τ' αὖ τρόνα, ποίκιλ' ἀθύρματα,
ἀργύρεα τ' ἀνάριθμα ποτήρια κἀλέφαις.'   10
ὣς εἶπ'· ὀτραλέως δ' ἀνόρουσε πάτηρ φίλος.
φάμα δ' ἦλθε κατὰ πτόλιν εὐρύχορον φίλοις·
αὔτικ' Ἰλίαδαι σατίναις ὐπ' ἐντρόχοις
ἆγον αἰμιόνοις· ἐπέβαινε δὲ παῖς ὄχλος

γυναίκων τ᾽ ἄμα παρθενίκαν τ᾽ ἀπαλοσφύρων·   15
χῶρις δ᾽ αὖ Περάμοιο θύγατρες [ἐπήισαν].
ἵπποις δ᾽ ἄνδρες ὕπαγον ὑπ᾽ ἄρ[ματα κάμπυλα]
πάντες ἤίθεοι . . . . . .

55c

[μύρρα κα]ὶ κασία λίβανός τ᾽ ὀνεμείχνυτο.
γύναικες δ᾽ ἐλέλυσδον ὄσαι προγενέστεραι,
πάντες δ᾽ ἄνδρες ἐπήρατον ἴαχον ὄρθιον
πάον᾽, ὀνκαλέοντες Ἐκάβολον εὐλύραν,
ὔμνην δ᾽ Ἔκτορα κἀνδρομάχαν θεοεικέλοις.

58

κατθάνοισα δὲ κείσῃ, οὐδ᾽ ἔτι τις μναμοσύνα σέθεν

ἔσσετ᾽ οὐδέποτ᾽ εἰς ὕστερον· οὐ γὰρ πεδέχεις ῥόδων
τῶν ἐκ Πιερίας, ἀλλ᾽ ἀφάνης κἠν Ἀίδα δόμῳ
φοιτάσεις πεδ᾽ ἀμαύρων νεκύων ἐκπεποταμένα.

88

πλήρης μὲν ἐφαίνετ᾽ ἀ σελάννα·
αἰ δ᾽ ὡς περὶ βῶμον ἐστάθησαν . . .

93

Κρῆσσαί νύ ποτ᾽ ὦδ᾽ ἐμμελέως πόδεσσιν
ὤρχηντ᾽ ἀπάλοισ᾽ ἀμφ᾽ ἐρόεντα βῶμον.

. . . .

πόας τέρεν ἄνθος μάλακον μάτεισαι

94

Δέδυκε μὲν ἀ σελάννα
καὶ Πληίαδες· μέσαι δέ
νύκτες, παρὰ δ᾽ ἔρχετ᾽ ὤρα·
ἔγω δὲ μόνα κατεύδω.

96

.   .   .   .

τεθνάκην δ' ἀδόλως θέλω.
  ἄ με ψισδομένα κατελίμπανεν
πόλλα καὶ τόδ' ἔειπ[ε μοι]·
‘ ὤμ' ὠς δεῖνα πεπόνθαμεν,   5
  Ψάπφ'· ἦ μάν σ' ἀέκοισ' ἀπυλιμπάνω'.
τὰν δ' ἔγω τάδ' ἀμειβόμαν·
‘ χαίροισ' ἔρχεο κἄμεθεν
  μέμναισ', οἶσθα γάρ, ὥς σε πεδήπομεν.
αἰ δὲ μή, ἀλλά σ' ἔγω θέλω   10

ὄμμναισαι, [σὺ δὲ] λάθεαι,
  ὄσ[σα μάλθακα] καὶ κάλ' ἐπάσχομεν·
π[όλλοις γὰρ στεφά]νοις ἴων
καὶ ϝρ[όδων κρο]κίων τ' ὔμοι
  καὶ . . παρ' ἔμοι παρεθήκαο   15
καὶ πό[λλαις ὑπα]θύμιδας
πλέκ[ταις ἀμφ' ἀ]πάλᾳ δέρᾳ
  ἀνθέων ἐ[ράτων] πεποημμέναις.
καὶ πόλλῳ [λιπάρως] μύρῳ
βρενθείῳ βασιληίῳ   20
  ἐξαλείψαο κα[λλίκομον κάρα] . . .

97

κατθάνην δ' ἴμερός τις [ἔχει με καί]
λωτίνοις δροσόεντας [ὄ-]
χ[θ]οις ἴδην Ἀχέρ[οντος . . .]

98

[. . . . . . ἀπὺ] Σαρδ[ίων]
  [. . . πόλ]λακι τυῖδε νῶν ἔχοισα.
ὠς π[εδεζ]ώομεν, β[εβάω]ς ἔχεν
σὲ θέᾳ ϝικέλαν ἀρι-
      γνωτᾳ, σᾷ δὲ μάλιστ' ἔχαιρε μόλπᾳ.   5

νῦν δὲ Λύδαισιν ἐμπρέπεται γυναί-
κεσσιν, ὥς ποτ᾽ ἀελίω
     δύντος ἀ ϝροδοδάκτυλος σελάννα
πάντα περρέχοισ᾽ ἄστρα, φάος δ᾽ ἐπί-
σχει θάλασσαν ἐπ᾽ ἀλμύραν   10
   ἴσως καὶ πολυανθέμοις ἀρούραις.
ἀ δ᾽ ἐέρσα κάλα κέχυται, τεθάλαισι δὲ ϝρόδα κἄπαλ᾽ ἄν-
     θρυσκα καὶ μελίλωτος ἀνθεμώδης.
πόλλα δὲ ζαφοίταισ᾽ ἀγάνας ἐπι-   15
μνάσθεισ᾽ Ἄτθιδος ἰμέρῳ
   λέπταν ποι φρένα, κῆρ δ᾽ ἄσᾳ βόρηται.
κήθυ δ᾽ ἔλθην ἄμμ᾽ ὄξυ βόᾳ, τὰ δ᾽ οὐ
νῶν τἄπυστα νὺξ πολύως
   γαρύε[ι δι᾽] ἄλος π[όρων . . .]   20

107

Κατθνάσκει, Κυθέρη᾽, ἄβρος Ἄδωνις· τί κε θεῖμεν;
καττύπτεσθε, κόραι, καὶ κατερείκεσθε χίτωνας.

114

Γλύκηα μᾶτερ, οὔ τοι δύναμαι κρέκην τὸν ἴστον
πόθῳ δάμεισα παῖδος ϝραδίναν δι᾽ Ἀφροδίταν.

116

οἶον τὸ γλυκύμαλον ἐρεύθεται ἄκρῳ ἐπ᾽ ὔσδῳ,
ἄκρον ἐπ᾽ ἀκροτάτῳ λελάθοντο δὲ μαλοδρόπηες,
οὐ μὰν ἐκλελάθοντ᾽, ἀλλ᾽ οὐκ ἐδύναντ᾽ ἐπίκεσθαι.

117

οἴαν τὰν ὑάκινθον ἐν οὔρεσι ποίμενες ἄνδρες
πόσσι καταστείβοισι, χάμαι δέ τε πόρφυρον ἄνθος
κάκκηται . . .

120

Ἔσπερε, πάντα φέρεις, ὅσα φαίνολις ἐσκέδασ' Αὔως,
φέρεις ὄιν,
φέρεις αἶγα, φέρεις ἄπυ μάτερι παῖδα.

121

ἦρος ἄγγελος ἱμερόφωνος ἀήδων

123

Ἴψοι δὴ τὸ μέλαθρον —
        Ὑμήναον —
ἀέρρατε, τέκτονες ἄνδρες·
        Ὑμήναον.
γάμβρος δ' ἴσος ἔρχετ' Ἄρευι —
        Ὑμήναον —
ἄνδρος μεγάλω πόλυ μέσδων·
        Ὑμήναον.

124

Θυρώρῳ πόδες ἐπτορόγυιοι,
τὰ δὲ σάμβαλα πεμπεβόηα,
πίσυγγοι δὲ δέκ' ἐξεπόναισαν.

127

τίω σ', ὦ φίλε γάμβρε, κάλως ἐικάσδω;
ὄρπακι ϝραδίνῳ σε μάλιστ' ἐικάσδω.

128

Ὄλβιε γάμβρε, σοὶ μὲν δὴ γάμος, ὡς ἄραο
ἐκτετέλεστ', ἔχεις δὲ πάρθενον ὡς ἄραο . . .
σοὶ χάριεν μὲν εἶδος, ὄππατα δ' ⟨ἐστὶ νύμφας⟩
μέλλιχ', ἔρος δ' ἐπ' ἱμέρτῳ κέχυται προσώπῳ
— ∪ ∪ — τετίμακ' ἔξοχά σ' Ἀφροδίτα.

137

Ἔρος δηὖτέ μ᾽ ὁ λυσιμέλης δόνει
γλυκύπικρον ἀμάχανον ὄρπετον . . .

149

Α΄. Θέλω τι ϝείπην, ἀλλά με κωλύει
αἴδως.
Β΄. Αἰ δ᾽ ἦχες ἔσλων ἴμερον ἢ κάλων,
καὶ μή τι ϝείπην γλῶσσ᾽ ἐκύκα κάκον,
αἴδως κε νῦν σ᾽ οὐκ ἦχεν ὄππατ᾽,
ἀλλ᾽ ἔλεγες περὶ τῶ δικαίως.

152

Ἔστι μοι κάλα πάϊς χρυσίοισιν ἀνθέμοισιν
ἐμφέρην ἔχοισα μόρφαν Κλεῦις ἀγαπάτα,
ἀντὶ τᾶς ἔγω οὐτε Λυδίαν παῖσαν οὐδ᾽ ἐράνναν . . .

IBYCUS

6

Ἦρι μὲν αἴ τε Κυδώνιαι
μαλίδες ἀρδόμεναι ῥόαι τ᾽
ἐκ ποταμῶν, ἵνα Παρθένων
κᾶπος ἀκήρατος, αἴ τ᾽ οἰνανθίδες
αὐξόμεναι σκιεροῖσιν ὑφ᾽ ἔρνεσιν   5
οἰναρέοις θαλέθοισιν. ἐμοὶ δ᾽ ἔρος
οὐδεμίαν κατάκοιτος ὥραν·
ἀλλ᾽ ἅθ᾽ ὑπὸ στεροπᾶς φλέγων
Θρηίκιος βορέας ἀίσ-
σων παρὰ Κύπριδος ἀζαλέαις μανί-   10
αισιν ἐρεμνὸς ἀθαμβής
ἐγκρατέως πεδόθεν τινάσσει
ἁμετέρας φρένας.

7

Ἔρος αὖτέ με κυανέοισιν ὑπο
βλεφάροις τακέρ᾿ ὄμμασι δερκόμενος
κηλήμασι παντοδαποῖσ᾿ ἐς ἄπειρα
δίκτυα Κύπριδι βάλλει.
ἦ μὰν τρομέω νιν ἐπερχόμενον,
ὥστε φερέζυγος ἵππος ἀεθλοφόρος ποτὶ γήρᾳ
ἀέκων σὺν ὄχεσφι θοοῖσ᾿ ἐς ἄμιλλαν ἔβα.

ANACREON

2

Ὦ ᾿ναξ, ᾧ δαμάλης Ἔρως
καὶ Νύμφαι κυανώπιδες
   πορφυρέη τ᾿ Ἀφροδίτη
συμπαίζουσιν, ἐπιστρέφεαι δ᾿
ὑψηλὰς ὀρέων κορυφάς,   5
γουνοῦμαί σε, σὺ δ᾿ εὐμενής
ἔλθ᾿ ἡμίν, κεχαρισμένης δ᾿
   εὐχωλῆς ἐπακούειν.
Κλευβούλῳ δ᾿ ἀγαθὸς γενεῦ
σύμβουλος, τὸν ἐμὸν δ᾿ ἔρωτ᾿,   10
   ὦ Δεύνυσε, δέχεσθαι.

4

Ὦ παῖ παρθένιον βλέπων,
δίζημαί σε, σὺ δ᾿ οὐ κλύεις
οὐκ εἰδώς, ὅτι τῆς ἐμῆς
   ψυχῆς ἡνιοχεύεις.

5

Σφαίρῃ δηῦτέ με πορφυρέῃ
βάλλων χρυσοκόμης Ἔρως
νήνι ποικιλοσαμβάλῳ
   συμπαίζειν προκαλεῖται.

ἢ δ᾿ — ἐστὶν γὰρ ἀπ᾿ εὐκτίτου   5
Λέσβου — τὴν μὲν ἐμὴν κόμην —
λευκὴ γάρ — καταμέμφεται,
  πρὸς δ᾿ ἄλλην τινὰ χάσκει.

34

            ἀστραγάλαι δ᾿ Ἔρωτός εἰσιν
μανίαι τε καὶ κυδοιμοί.

39

ἀγανῶς οἷά τε νεβρὸν νεοθηλέα
γαλαθηνόν, ὅς τ᾿ ἐν ὕλῃ κεροέσσης
ἀπολειφθεὶς ἀπὸ μητρὸς ἐπτοήθη . . .

44

Πολιοὶ μὲν ἡμὶν ἤδη
κρόταφοι κάρη τε λευκόν,
χαρίεσσα δ᾿ οὐκέτ᾿ ἥβη
πάρα, γηράλεοι δ᾿ ὀδόντες.
γλυκεροῦ δ᾿ οὐκέτι πολλός   5
βιότου χρόνος λέλειπται.
διὰ ταῦτ᾿ ἀνασταλύζω
θαμὰ Τάρταρον δεδοικώς.
Ἀίδεω γάρ ἐστι δεινὸς
μυχός, ἀργαλέη δ᾿ ἐς αὐτόν   10
κάτοδος· καὶ γὰρ ἑτοῖμον
καταβάντι μὴ ἀναβῆναι.

53

           <Ἔρως, ὅς> μ᾿ ἐσιδὼν γένειον
ὑποπόλιον χρυσοφαέννων πτερύγων ἀήταις
παραπέτεται.

88

Πῶλε Θρηκίη, τί δή με λοξὸν ὄμμασιν βλέπουσα
νηλεῶς φεύγεις, δοκεῖς δέ μ᾿ οὐδὲν εἰδέναι σοφόν;

ἴσθι τοι, καλῶς μὲν ἄν τοι τὸν χαλινὸν ἐμβάλοιμι,
ἡνίας δ᾽ ἔχων στρέφοιμί σ᾽ ἀμφὶ τέρματα δρόμου.
νῦν δὲ λειμῶνάς τε βόσκεαι κοῦφά τε σκιρτῶσα παίζεις·
δεξιὸν γὰρ ἱπποπείρην οὐκ ἔχεις ἐπεμβάτην.

101

Καρτερὸς ἐν πολέμοις Τιμόκριτος, οὗ τόδε σᾶμα·
Ἄρης δ᾽ οὐκ ἀγαθῶν φείδεται, ἀλλὰ κακῶν.

SIMONIDES

4

Ἄνδρ᾽ ἀγαθὸν μὲν ἀλαθέως γενέσθαι   στρ. α΄
χαλεπόν, χερσίν τε καὶ ποσὶ καὶ νόῳ
  τετράγωνον, ἄνευ ψόγου τετυγμένον·   3

. . . .

οὐδέ μοι ἐμμελέως τὸ Πιττάκειον   στρ. β΄
νέμεται, καίτοι σοφοῦ παρὰ φωτὸς εἰ-
  ρημένον· χαλεπὸν φάτ᾽ ἐσθλὸν ἔμμεναι.
θεὸς ἂν μόνος τοῦτ᾽ ἔχοι γέρας, ἄνδρα δ᾽ οὐκ
  ἔστι μὴ οὐ κακὸν ἔμμεναι,   15
ὅν ἀμάχανος συμφορὰ καθέλῃ.
πράξας γὰρ εὖ πᾶς ἀνὴρ ἀγαθός,
κακὸς δ᾽ εἰ κακῶς τι,
κἀπὶ πλεῖστον ἄριστοι
οὕς κε θεοὶ φιλῶσιν.   20
τοὔνεκεν οὔποτ᾽ ἐγὼ τὸ μὴ γενέσθαι   στρ. γ΄
δυνατὸν διζήμενος κενεὰν ἐς ἄ-
  πρακτον ἐλπίδα μοῖραν αἰῶνος βαλέω,
πανάμωμον ἄνθρωπον, εὐρυεδοῦς ὅσοι
  καρπὸν αἰνύμεθα χθονός.   25
ἐπί τ᾽ ὕμμιν εὑρὼν ἀπαγγελέω.
πάντας δ᾽ ἐπαίνημι καὶ φιλέω,

ἑκὼν ὅστις ἔρδῃ
μηδὲν αἰσχρόν· ἀνάγκᾳ δ'
οὐδὲ θεοὶ μάχονται.   30

. . . .   στρ. δ'

οὐκ ἐγὼ φιλόμωμος· ἐξαρκεῖ γ' ἐμοί
ὅ τε μὴ κακὸς μηδ' ἄγαν ἀπάλαμνος, εἰ-
    δώς γ' ὀνησίπολιν δίκαν,   35
ὑγιὴς ἀνήρ· οὐδὲ μή μιν ἐγώ
μωμήσομαι· τῶν γὰρ ἠλιθίων
ἀπείρων γενέθλα·
πάντα τοι κάλα, τοῖσι τ'
αἰσχρὰ μὴ μέμεικται.   40

5

        τῶν ἐν Θερμοπύλαισι θανόντων
εὐκλεὴς μὲν ἁ τύχα, καλὸς δ' ὁ πότμος,
βωμὸς δ' ὁ τάφος, πρὸ γόων δὲ μνᾶστις, ὁ δ' οἶκτος ἔπαινος.
ἐντάφιον δὲ τοιοῦτον
εὐρὼς οὔθ' ὁ πανδαμάτωρ ἀμαυρώσει χρόνος·   5
ἀνδρῶν δ' ἀγαθῶν ὅδε σηκὸς οἰκέταν εὐδοξίαν
Ἑλλάδος εἵλετο. μαρτυρεῖ δὲ καὶ Λεωνίδας,
κόσμον ὁ Σπάρτας βασιλεύς ἀρετᾶς μέγαν λελοιπώς
ἀέναόν τε κλέος.

6

ἄνθρωπος ἐὼν μή ποτε φάσῃς ὅτι γίνεται αὔριον,
μηδ' ἄνδρα ἰδὼν ὄλβιον, ὅσσον χρόνον ἔσσεται·
ὠκεῖα γὰρ οὐδὲ τανυπτερύγου μυίας
οὕτως ἁ μετάστασις.

7

οὐδὲ γὰρ οἳ πρότερόν ποτ' ἐπέλοντο,
θεῶν δ' ἐξ ἀνάκτων ἐγένονθ' υἷες ἡμίθεοι,
ἄπονον οὐδ' ἄφθιτον οὐδ' ἀκίνδυνον βίον
ἐς γῆρας ἐξίκοντο τελέσσαντες.

8

πάντα γὰρ μίαν ἱκνεῖται δασπλῆτα χάρυβδιν,
αἱ μεγάλαι τ᾽ ἀρεταὶ καὶ ὁ πλοῦτος . . .

9

Ἀνθρώπων ὀλίγον μέν
κάρτος, ἄπρακτοι δὲ μεληδόνες, αἰῶνι δ᾽ ἐν παύρῳ πόνος ἀμφὶ
   πόνῳ.
ὁ δ᾽ ἄφυκτος ὅμως ἐπικρέμαται θάνατος·
κεῖνοι γὰρ ἴσον λάχον μέρος οἵ τ᾽ ἀγαθοί
ὅστις τε κακός . . .

13

ὅτε

λάρνακι ἐν δαιδαλέᾳ
ἄνεμός τέτμε πνέων
κινηθεῖσά τε λίμνα,
δείματι ἤριπεν οὔ τ᾽ ἀδιάντοισι παρειαῖς,   5
ἀμφί τε Περσεῖ βάλεν φίλαν χέρ᾽ εἶπέ τ᾽· ʽ Ὦ τέκος,
οἷον ἔχω πόνον·
σὺ δ᾽ ἀωτεῖς· γαλαθηνῷ τ᾽
ἤτορι κνώσσεις ἐν ἀτερπεῖ
δούρατι χαλκεογόμφῳ,   10
νυκτιλαμπεῖ κυανέῳ τε δνόφῳ ταθείς.
ἅλμαν δ᾽ ὕπερθεν τεᾶν κομᾶν βαθεῖαν
παριόντος κύματος οὐκ
ἀλέγεις οὐδ᾽ ἀνέμου φθόγγον πορφυρέᾳ κείμενος
ἐν χλανίδι προσέχων καλὸν πρόσωπον.   15
εἰ δέ τοι δεινὸν τό γε δεινὸν ἦν, καί κεν
ἐμῶν ῥημάτων λεπτὸν ὑπεῖχες οὖας.
κέλομ᾽, εὖδε, βρέφος, εὑδέτω δὲ πόντος, εὑδέτω δ᾽
ἄμετρον κακόν· μεταβουλία δέ τις φανείη,
Ζεῦ πάτερ, ἐκ σέο.
ὅτι δὴ θαρσαλέον ἔπος   21
εὔχομαι καὶ νόσφι δίκας, σύγγνωθί μοι.᾽

48

τίς κεν αἰνήσειε, νόῳ πίσυνος Λίνδου ναέταν Κλεόβουλον
ἀενάοις ποταμοῖσ᾿ ἄνθεσί τ᾿ εἰαρινοῖς
ἀελίου τε φλογὶ χρυσέας τε σελάνας
καὶ θαλασσίαισι δίναισ᾿ ἀντία θέντα μένος
στάλας;   5
ἅπαντα γάρ ἐστι θεῶν ἥσσω· λίθον δέ
καὶ βρότεοι παλάμαι θραύοντι· μωροῦ φωτὸς ἅδε βουλά.

53

πόλις ἄνδρα διδάσκει.

83

Μνῆμα τόδε κλεινοῖο Μεγιστία, ὅν ποτε Μῆδοι
    Σπερχειὸν ποταμὸν κτεῖναν ἀμειψάμενοι,
μάντιος, ὃς τότε Κῆρας ἐπερχομένας σάφα εἰδώς
    οὐκ ἔτλη Σπάρτης ἡγεμόνας προλιπεῖν.

84

Σῆμα καταφθιμένοιο Μεγακλέος εὖτ᾿ ἄν ἴδωμαι,
    οἰκτίρω σέ, τάλαν Καλλία, οἷ ἔπαθες.

85

᾿Ανδρὸς ἀριστεύσαντος ἐν ῾Ελλάδι τῶν ἐφ᾿ ἑαυτοῦ
    ῾Ιππίου ᾿Αρχεδίκην ἥδε κέκευθε κόνις·
ἥ πατρός τε καὶ ἀνδρὸς ἀδελφῶν τ᾿ οὖσα τυράννων
    παίδων τ᾿, οὐκ ἤρθη νοῦν ἐς ἀτασθαλίην.

88

῾Ελλήνων προμαχοῦντες ᾿Αθηναῖοι Μαραθῶνι
    χρυσοφόρων Μήδων ἐστόρεσαν δύναμιν.

91

Μυριάσιν ποτὲ τῇδε τριακοσίαισ᾿ ἐμάχοντο
    ἐκ Πελοποννάσου χιλιάδες τέτορες.

92

Ὦ ξεῖν᾽, ἀγγέλλειν Λακεδαιμονίοισ᾽, ὅτι τῇδε
κείμεθα τοῖς κείνων ῥήμασι πειθόμενοι.

105

Ἑλλήνων ἀρχηγὸς ἐπεὶ στρατὸν ὤλεσε Μήδων
Παυσανίας, Φοίβῳ μνῆμ᾽ ἀνέθηκε τόδε.

118

Εἰ τὸ καλῶς θνήσκειν ἀρετῆς μέρος ἐστὶ μέγιστον,
ἡμῖν ἐκ πάντων τοῦτ᾽ ἀπένειμε Τύχη·
Ἑλλάδι γὰρ σπεύδοντες ἐλευθερίην περιθεῖναι
κείμεθ᾽ ἀγηράντῳ χρώμενοι εὐλογίῃ.

121

Ἄσβεστον κλέος οἵδε φίλῃ περὶ πατρίδι θέντες
κυάνεον θανάτου ἀμφεβάλοντο νέφος·
οὐ δὲ τεθνᾶσι θανόντες, ἐπεί σφ᾽ ἀρετὴ καθύπερθεν
κυδαίνουσ᾽ ἀνάγει δώματος ἐξ Ἀίδεω.

135

Σῶμα μὲν ἀλλοδαπὴ κεύθει κόνις, ἐν δέ σε πόντῳ,
Κλείσθενες, Εὐξείνῳ μοῖρ᾽ ἔκιχεν θανάτου
πλαζόμενον· γλυκεροῦ δὲ μελίφρονος οἴκαδε νόστου
ἤμπλακες, οὐδ᾽ ἵκευ Χῖον ἐς ἀμφιρύτην.

138

Κρὴς γενεὰν Βρόταχος Γορτύνιος ἐνθάδε κεῖμαι
οὐ κατὰ τοῦτ᾽ ἐλθών, ἀλλὰ κατ᾽ ἐμπορίαν.

142

Ἦ σεῦ καὶ φθιμένας λεύκ᾽ ὀστέα τῷδ᾽ ἐνὶ τύμβῳ
ἴσκω ἔτι τρομέειν θῆρας, ἄγρωσσα Λυκάς.
τὰν δ᾽ ἀρετὰν οἶδεν μέγα Πήλιον ἅ τ᾽ ἀρίδηλος
Ὄσσα Κιθαιρῶνός τ᾽ οἰονόμοι σκοπιαί.

PINDAR

OLYMPIA XIV

ΑΣΩΠΙΧΩΙ ΟΡΧΟΜΕΝΙΩΙ ΣΤΑΔΙΕΙ

Καφισίων ὑδάτων   στρ. α΄
λαχοῖσαν αἵτε ναίετε καλλίπωλον ἕδραν,
ὦ λιπαρᾶς ἀοίδιμοι βασίλειαι
Χάριτες Ἐρχομενοῦ, παλαιγόνων Μινυᾶν ἐπίσκοποι,
κλῦτ᾽, ἐπεὶ εὔχομαι. σὺν γὰρ ὔμμιν τὰ τερπνὰ καὶ   5
τὰ γλυκέ᾽ ἄνεται πάντα βροτοῖς,
εἰ σοφός, εἰ καλός, εἴ τις ἀγλαὸς ἀνήρ.
οὐδὲ γὰρ θεοὶ σεμνᾶν Χαρίτων ἄτερ
κοιρανέοντι χοροὺς οὔτε δαῖτας· ἀλλὰ πάντων ταμίαι
ἔργων ἐν οὐρανῷ, χρυσότοξον θέμεναι πάρα   10
Πύθιον Ἀπόλλωνα θρόνους,
αἰέναον σέβοντι πατρὸς Ὀλυμπίοιο τιμάν.

⟨ὦ⟩ πότνι᾽ Ἀγλαΐα   στρ. β΄
φιλησίμολπέ τ᾽ Εὐφροσύνα, θεῶν κρατίστου
παῖδες, ἐπακοοῖτε νῦν, Θαλία τε   15
ἐρασίμολπε, ἰδοῖσα τόνδε κῶμον ἐπ᾽ εὐμενεῖ τύχᾳ
κοῦφα βιβῶντα· Λυδῷ γὰρ Ἀσώπιχον τρόπῳ
ἐν μελέταις τ᾽ ἀείδων ἔμολον,
οὕνεκ᾽ Ὀλυμπιόνικος ἁ Μινύεια
σεῦ ἕκατι. μελαντειχέα νῦν δόμον   20
Φερσεφόνας ἴθι, Ἀχοῖ, πατρὶ κλυτὰν φέροισ᾽ ἀγγελίαν,
Κλεόδαμον ὄφρ᾽ ἰδοῖσ᾽, υἱὸν εἴπῃς ὅτι οἱ νέαν
κόλποις παρ᾽ εὐδόξοις Πίσας
ἐστεφάνωσε κυδίμων ἀέθλων πτεροῖσι χαίταν.

ISTHMIA VII

ΣΤΡΕΨΙΑΔΗΙ ΘΗΒΑΙΩΙ ΠΑΓΚΡΑΤΙΩΙ

Τίνι τῶν πάρος, ὦ μάκαιρα Θήβα,   στρ. α′
καλῶν ἐπιχωρίων μάλιστα θυμὸν τεὸν
εὔφρανας; ἦρα χαλκοκρότου πάρεδρον
Δαμάτερος ἀνίκ᾽ εὐρυχαίταν
ἄντειλας Διόνυσον, ἢ χρυσῷ μεσονύκτιον   5
     νείφοντα δεξαμένα
τὸν φέρτατον θεῶν,   5b

ὁπότ᾽ Ἀμφιτρύωνος ἐν θυρέτροις   ἀντ. α′
σταθεὶς ἄλοχον μετῆλθεν Ἡρακλείοις γοναῖς;
ἦτ᾽ ἀμφὶ πυκναῖς Τειρεσίαο βουλαῖς;
ἦτ᾽ ἀμφ᾽ Ἰόλαον ἱππόμητιν;
ἢ Σπαρτῶν ἀκαμαντολογχᾶν; ἢ ὅτε καρτερᾶς   10
    Ἄδραστον ἐξ ἀλαλᾶς
ἄμπεμψας ὀρφανὸν   10b

μυρίων ἑτάρων ἐς Ἄργος ἵππιον;   ἐπ. α′
ἢ Δωρίδ᾽ ἀποικίαν οὕνεκεν ὀρθῷ
ἔστασας ἐπὶ σφυρῷ
Λακεδαιμονίων, ἕλον δ᾽ Ἀμύκλας
Αἰγεῖδαι σέθεν ἔκγονοι, μαντεύμασι Πυθίοις;   15
ἀλλὰ παλαιὰ γὰρ
εὕδει χάρις, ἀμνάμονες δὲ βροτοί,

ὅ τι μὴ σοφίας ἄωτον ἄκρον   στρ. β′
κλυταῖς ἐπέων ῥοαῖσιν ἐξίκηται ζυγέν.
κώμαζ᾽ ἔπειτεν ἁδυμελεῖ σὺν ὕμνῳ   20
καὶ Στρεψιάδᾳ· φέρει γὰρ Ἰσθμοῖ
νίκαν παγκρατίου σθένει τ᾽ ἔκπαγλος ἰδεῖν τε μορ-
     φάεις· ἄγει τ᾽ ἀρετὰν
οὐκ αἴσχιον φυᾶς.   22b

φλέγεται δὲ ἰοπλόκοισι Μοίσαις,   ἀντ. β'
μάτρωΐ θ' ὁμωνύμῳ δέδωκε κοινὸν θάλος,
χάλκασπις ᾧ πότμον μὲν "Αρης ἔμειξεν,   25
τιμὰ δ' ἀγαθοῖσιν ἀντίκειται.
ἴστω γὰρ σαφές, ὅστις ἐν ταύτᾳ νεφέλᾳ χάλα-
    ζαν αἵματος πρὸ φίλας
πάτρας ἀμύνεται,   27b

λοιγὸν ἄντα φέρων ἐναντίῳ στρατῷ,   ἐπ. β'
ἀστῶν γενεᾷ μέγιστον κλέος αὔξων
ζώων τ' ἀπὸ καὶ θανών.   30
τὺ δέ, Διοδότοιο παῖ, μαχατὰν
αἰνέων Μελέαγρον, αἰνέων δὲ καὶ "Εκτορα
Ἀμφιάραόν τε,
εὐανθέ' ἀπέπνευσας ἁλικίαν

προμάχων ἀν' ὅμιλον, ἔνθ' ἄριστοι   στρ. γ'
ἔσχον πολέμοιο νεῖκος ἐσχάταις ἐλπίσιν.   36
ἔτλαν δὲ πένθος οὐ φατόν· ἀλλὰ νῦν μοι
Γαιάοχος εὐδίαν ὄπασσεν
ἐκ χειμῶνος. ἀείσομαι χαίταν στεφάνοισιν ἁρ-
    μόζων. ὁ δ' ἀθανάτων
μὴ θρασσέτω φθόνος.   39b

ὅ τι τερπνὸν ἐπάμερον διώκων   ἀντ. γ'
ἔκαλος ἔπειμι γῆρας ἔς τε τὸν μόρσιμον   41
αἰῶνα. θνᾴσκομεν γὰρ ὁμῶς ἅπαντες·
δαίμων δ' ἄϊσος· τὰ μακρὰ δ' εἴ τις
παπταίνει, βραχὺς ἐξικέσθαι χαλκόπεδον θεῶν
    ἕδραν· ὅ τοι πτερόεις
ἔρριψε Πάγασος   44b

δεσπόταν ἐθέλοντ' ἐς οὐρανοῦ σταθμοὺς   ἐπ. γ'
ἐλθεῖν μεθ' ὁμάγυριν Βελλεροφόνταν   46
Ζηνός. τὸ δὲ πὰρ δίκαν

γλυκὺ πικροτάτα μένει τελευτά.
ἄμμι δ᾽, ὦ χρυσέᾳ κόμᾳ θάλλων, πόρε, Λοξία,
τεαῖσιν ἀμίλλαισιν
εὐανθέα καὶ Πυθόϊ στέφανον.

50

64

Ὦ ταὶ λιπαραὶ καὶ ἰοστέφανοι καὶ ἀοίδιμοι,
Ἑλλάδος ἔρεισμα, κλειναὶ Ἀθᾶναι,
δαιμόνιον πτολίεθρον.

SCOLIA

1

Παλλὰς Τριτογένει᾽, ἄνασσ᾽ Ἀθάνα,
ὄρθου τήνδε πόλιν τε καὶ πολίτας
ἄτερ ἀλγέων καὶ στάσεων
καὶ θανάτων ἀώρων, σύ τε καὶ πατήρ.

6

Εἴθ᾽ ἐξῆν, ὁποῖός τις ἦν ἕκαστος,
τὸ στῆθος διελόντ᾽, ἔπειτα τὸν νοῦν
ἐσιδόντα, κλείσαντα πάλιν,
ἄνδρα φίλον νομίζειν ἀδόλῳ φρενί.

7

Ὑγιαίνειν μὲν ἄριστον ἀνδρὶ θνατῷ,
δεύτερον δὲ φυὰν καλὸν γενέσθαι,
τὸ τρίτον δὲ πλουτεῖν ἀδόλως
καὶ τὸ τέταρτον ἡβᾶν μετὰ τῶν φίλων.

10

Ἐν μύρτου κλαδὶ τὸ ξίφος φορήσω,
ὥσπερ Ἁρμόδιος καὶ Ἀριστογείτων,

ὅτε τὸν τύραννον κτανέτην
ἰσονόμους τ᾽ Ἀθήνας ἐποιησάτην.

11

Φίλταθ᾽ Ἁρμόδι᾽, οὔ τί που τέθνηκας,
νήσοις δ᾽ ἐν μακάρων σέ φασιν εἶναι,
ἵνα περ ποδώκης Ἀχιλεύς
Τυδείδην τέ φασιν ἐσθλὸν Διομήδεα.

17

Εἴθε λύρα καλὴ γενοίμην ἐλεφαντίνη
καί με καλοὶ παῖδες φοροῖεν Διονύσιον ἐς χορόν.

18

Εἴθ᾽ ἄπυρον καλὸν γενοίμην μέγα χρυσίον
καί με καλὴ γυνὴ φοροίη καθαρὸν θεμένη νόον.

19

Σύν μοι πῖνε, συνήβα, συνέρα, συστεφανηφόρει,
σύν μοι μαινομένῳ μαίνεο, σὺν σώφρονι σωφρόνει.

AESCHYLUS

2

Κυανέη καὶ τούσδε μενεγχέας ὤλεσεν ἄνδρας
    Μοῖρα, πολύρρηνον πατρίδα ῥυομένους.
ζωὸν δὲ φθιμένων πέλεται κλέος, οἵ ποτε γυίοις
    τλήμονες Ὀσσαίαν ἀμφιέσαντο κόνιν.

3

Αἰσχύλον Εὐφορίωνος Ἀθηναῖον τόδε κεύθει
    μνῆμα καταφθίμενον πυροφόροιο Γέλας.
ἀλκὴν δ᾽ εὐδόκιμον Μαραθώνιον ἄλσος ἂν εἴποι
    καὶ βαθυχαιτήεις Μῆδος ἐπιστάμενος.

PLATO

4

Ἀστέρας εἰσαθρεῖς, Ἀστὴρ ἐμός· εἴθε γενοίμην
οὐρανός, ὡς πολλοῖσ᾽ ὄμμασιν εἰς σὲ βλέπω.

5

Ἀστὴρ πρὶν μὲν ἔλαμπες ἐνὶ ζῳοῖσιν Ἑῷος,
νῦν δὲ θανὼν λάμπεις Ἕσπερος ἐν φθιμένοις.

10

Οἵδε ποτ᾽ Αἰγαίοιο βαρύβρομον οἶδμα λιπόντες
Ἐκβατάνων πεδίῳ κείμεθ᾽ ἐνὶ μεσάτῳ.
χαῖρε κλυτή ποτε πατρὶς Ἐρέτρια, χαίρετ᾽ Ἀθῆναι,
γείτονες Εὐβοίης, χαῖρε θάλασσα φίλη.

NOTES

ELEGIAC AND IAMBIC POETRY

The elegiac couplet consists essentially of two dactylic hexameters. The first is simply the familiar Homeric line

$$- \cup \cup \mid - \cup \cup \mid - \cup \cup \mid - \cup \cup \mid - \cup \cup \mid - -;$$

the second is shortened by the omission of half the third foot and half the sixth foot:

$$- \cup \cup \mid - \cup \cup \mid - \parallel - \cup \cup \mid - \cup \cup \mid -.$$

The two halves of the second line are thought of as being separate; no word ever continues from the third foot into the fourth. A spondee may be substituted for a dactyl anywhere except in the last half of the second line; but that half-line always preserves the pattern $- \cup \cup - \cup \cup -$.

To us the word 'elegy' connotes a lament; and some of the most famous poems in this metre are laments. But the oldest elegiac poems which we have are not laments, at any rate not laments for the dead; they are poems of military exhortation, or songs to be sung at feasts. Elegiac poems appear to have been sung to the accompaniment of the flute. The diction of the earliest ones follows closely that of the epic.

CALLINUS flourished at Ephesus in the middle of the 7th century B.C.

1. The poet addresses a group of young men, and stirs them up to help their neighbors against the enemy.

1. τεῦ is Ionic for τίνος, and κότε is Ionic for πότε. —κατάκεισθε can mean simply 'lie idle', but it could also mean 'lie feasting'; perhaps we should visualize the poet addressing the young men at a banquet.

2, 3. ἀμφιπερικτίονας is the object of αἰδεῖσθε, 'don't you feel shame before your neighbors?', and μεθιέντες is intransitive, 'being so idle'.

4. πόλεμος means 'war' here; but in line 11 it has the regular Homeric sense of 'battle'. After this line at least one line must be missing, since the next line should be a full hexameter.

5. ὕστατ' ἀκοντισάτω means 'hurl his last', 'make a last throw'. ὕστατα is the so-called cognate or inner accusative. Callinus expects a great deal of a man; even a death wound is no excuse for relaxing one's efforts.

7. πέρι is for ὑπέρ, as frequently in Homer.

11. ἔλσας is from εἴλω, 'roll up', 'pack close'. Translate 'mustering up a stout heart'.

12. κως is Ionic for πως. Take ἄνδρα as the subject of φυγεῖν, and εἰμαρμένον (perfect participle of μείρομαι) as subject of the sentence. 'It is not fated that a man should in any way escape death . . .'

13. οὐδ' εἰ: 'not even if'. — προγόνων, 'ancestors', is genitive of source; and γένος is accusative of limitation: 'in respect to his birth'.

14. φυγών means 'fleeing from', not merely 'surviving'.

15. ἔρχεται: 'comes back'; κίχεν is gnomic aorist.

17. He is mourned by high and low, (μέγας and ὀλίγος respectively).

19. ζώων is Ionic for ζάων.

TYRTAEUS lived at Sparta and wrote elegies there at the time of the Second Messenian War (about 635 B.C.) There is a tradition that he was an immigrant to Sparta, a lame Athenian schoolmaster; but this tradition need not be believed.

2. This is a fragment of a poem called Εὐνομίη, which dealt with good order in the Spartan state. These lines are a reminiscence of the Dorian migration to the Peloponnesus from the tetrapolis in Doris, of which Erineus (line 3) was one of the four cities.

6, 7. This poem has two distinct themes; in fact it has been thought to be two separate poems. In lines 1–14 the poet dwells

on the misery of exile which follows defeat in war; lines 15–32
urge the young men of Sparta not to leave the brunt of battle
to the old, since the spectacle of an old man's corpse lying on
the battlefield is pitiful and ugly, but the body of a young man
(the poet maintains) is beautiful, however much it may be
disfigured.

9. ἐλέγχει, strengthened by κατά, means 'give the lie to'. The
exile's record belies his prepossessing appearance.

16. φόβου: 'rout'.

20. γεραιούς must be scanned ⌣ ⌣ —. The shortening of αι
before the succeeding vowel-sound is easy.

21ff. These lines are a close adaptation of a passage in
Homer (*Iliad* 23, 71–6). Priam begs Hector not to face Achilles, because he foresees that his son will be killed and Troy
taken and sacked, and his own body mangled by the dogs. He
concludes:

> νέῳ δέ τε πάντ' ἐπέοικεν
> ἀρηϊκταμένῳ, δεδαϊγμένῳ ὀξέϊ χαλκῷ,
> κεῖσθαι· πάντα δὲ καλὰ θανόντι περ, ὅττι φανήῃ.
> ἀλλ' ὅτε δὴ πολιόν τε κάρη πολιόν τε γένειον
> αἰδῶ τ' αἰσχύνωσι κύνες κταμένοιο γέροντος,
> τοῦτο δὴ οἴκτιστον πέλεται δειλοῖσι βροτοῖσιν.

'For a young man it is altogether appropriate, when he is slain in
war and pierced by the sharp bronze, for his body to lie exposed;
though he is dead all is handsome, whatever is seen. But for dogs to
disfigure the grey head and grey beard of an old man slain, and
mutilate his sexual organs, is surely the most pitiful thing that can
happen among wretched men.'

Priam, in order to strengthen his plea, dwells on the indignities
he may expect to suffer, and as these present themselves more
and more vividly to his imagination, he passionately adds one
horror to another, so that his speech, while painful, is moving
and full of pathos. The idea and several of the details are con-
scientiously reproduced here, but they suffer when rendered by
the coarse and strident muse of Tyrtaeus. He searches in cold

blood for something with which to produce a shocking effect. The result can only be called grotesque. It is also worth noticing that Priam is not suggesting that a young man should go out and die in his stead. Altogether this is not a very happy adaptation. Virgil remarked that it is easier to steal his club from Hercules than a line from Homer.

26. τά is demonstrative. — ἰδεῖν: limiting infinitive with αἰσχρά and νεμεσητόν. Notice how many times he insists on underlining his point.

27. χρόα is accusative of limitation (from χρώς).

31. εὖ διαβάς: 'with legs set well apart'.

8. 1. ἀλλά goes with θαρσεῖτε: 'But come, take heart'. ἀνικήτου is not 'unconquered' but 'invincible'.

2. 'Zeus doesn't yet hold his neck aslant.' This is meant to be reassuring, though it's difficult to see why. When a Greek meant 'no', he didn't shake his head, as we do; he bridled like a horse. In such an attitude Zeus might be said to hold his neck aslant.

5. θέμενος: 'counting'.

7. ἀίδηλα: probably in its active sense, 'destructive'. The point of this and the following lines is that war is disagreeable in any case, but much more disagreeable if you are routed than if you stand firm. The greatest losses in hoplite battles generally occurred when the line broke, so that each man no longer covered his neighbor's flank.

8. ὀργή, when applied to persons, means their 'temper' or 'disposition'. Probably πολέμου is felt to be more or less personified here.

10. 'You have pushed on to the point of satiety of both.'

16. ἢν αἰσχρὰ πάθῃ: 'if he suffers disgrace'; but the context shows that this phrase is a euphemism for 'if he acts disgracefully', by running away.

17. ὄπισθε modifies δαΐζειν.

19. κακκείμενος = κατακείμενος.

20. νῶτον is accusative of limitation; 'in the back'.

28. ἑστάτω: second perfect imperative of ἵστημι. This form is intransitive and means 'let him have set himself', or more simply, 'let him stand'.

31. πάρ: from παρά, by apocope.

32. ἐν: 'moreover'.

33. πεπλημένος: from πελάζω.

36. πτώσσοντες: 'crouching'.

9. This poem expounds the strictly military ideal of the Spartan state.

1. ἐν λόγῳ τιθείην: 'take any account of'.

2. ἀρετῆς: genitive of cause. ἀρετή is any kind of excellence.

3. οὐδ' εἰ is the contrary of καὶ εἰ: 'not even if'.

4. θέων: participle of θέω.

5. Tithonus was the husband of the Dawn.

6. Midas' touch turned everything to gold. Cinyras was a proverbially wealthy king of Cyprus. μάλιον, found only here, = μᾶλλον.

7. βασιλεύτερος: 'more kingly'. Pelops, son of Tantalus, was king of Mycenae, and grandfather of Agamemnon.

8. Adrastus was one of the Seven against Thebes; he was an old man, temperate, wise, and eloquent.

9. This line summarizes the foregoing. Only ἀλκή matters.

12. δηΐων ὀρέγοιτο: 'reach out after the enemy'. Verbs of touching, aiming at, etc. take the genitive.

16. ὅστις ἀνήρ: 'if a man, etc.'

17. ἐπί is an adverb which merely strengthens λάθηται.

18. παρθέμενος: 'staking', 'hazarding'.

21. ἔτρεψε: gnomic aorist.

22. ἔσχεθε: 'he checks'. Also gnomic aorist.

25–6. Honorable wounds, in front; and notice how many it takes to kill him!

27. The δέ should be omitted in translation; the grammar of the elegists is sometimes paratactic, like that of Homer.

38. Ἀίδην: here the place, not the god, as generally in Homer.

40. βλάπτειν αἰδοῦς: 'deprive him of due respect'. The genitive is explained as a genitive of separation. Compare *Odyssey* 1, 195: τόν γε θεοὶ βλάπτουσι κελεύθου.

41. οἵ τε κατ' αὐτόν: 'those of his own age'.

44. μεθιεὶς πολέμου: 'relaxing from war'.

MIMNERMUS lived at Colophon in the second half of the seventh century. His themes are the sweetness and brevity of youth, and the horror of old age, which he says is worse than death.

1. 2. μέλοι: optative by assimilation.

6. ὅ τε: omit τε in translation — more parataxis. — αἰσχρὸν ὁμῶς καὶ κακόν: 'alike ugly and wretched'. — τιθεῖ (an Ionic form): 'makes'.

7. ἀμφί is adverbial. — φρένας is accusative of limitation.

9. παισίν: 'boys'. He is an unwelcome lover to both boys and women.

10. ἔθηκε: 'made'.

2. This poem begins with a reminiscence of Glaucus' reply to Diomedes (*Iliad* 6, 146)

> οἵη περ φύλλων γενεή, τοίη δὲ καὶ ἀνδρῶν.
> φύλλα τὰ μέν τ' ἄνεμος χαμάδις χέει, ἄλλα δέ θ' ὕλη
> τηλεθόωσα φύει, ἔαρος δ' ἐπιγίγνεται ὥρη.
> ὡς ἀνδρῶν γενεὴ ἡ μὲν φύει, ἡ δ' ἀπολήγει.

"How vain it is to boast of one's lineage," Glaucus means to say, "when one generation succeeds another so swiftly — like to the generation of leaves, so also is that of men . . ." But Mimnermus makes of the exfoliation of leaves in springtime a symbol of the brief joys of youth; the shortness of this present season is what he grieves for.

1. οἷά τε φύλλα is resumed by τοῖσι in line 3.

3. πήχυιον ἐπὶ χρόνον: 'for a cubit of time', not long. πήχυιον is an adjective formed from πῆχυς, 'cubit'.

4. πρὸς θεῶν: 'at the hands of the gods'.

8. ὅσον is used here of time, 'so long as'.

9, 10. 'But when this consummation of the good season is past, then at once it becomes better to die than live.' —παρα-μείψεται is the Homeric short-vowel aorist subjunctive.

11. οἶκος: 'property'.

4. Tithonus was the mortal husband of the Dawn. She asked for and obtained the gift of immortality for him, but she forgot to add the stipulation that he should remain always young.

2. καί: 'even'.

5. 2. ὁμηλικίη means 'those in the same time of life', and especially 'those who are young together'.

3. ὤφελεν: second aorist of ὀφείλω, 'it ought to have been longer', hence 'I wish it were longer!'

6. 1. αἲ γάρ introduces a wish.

2. ἑξηκονταετῆ agrees with με understood. Solon made a reply to this poem (Solon fragment 22).

10. The poet pities the Sun-god for his labors.

1. ἔλλαχεν: epic second aorist of λαγχάνω.

2. κοτε is Ionic for ποτε. — ἄμπαυσις = ἀνάπαυσις.

3. ἐπεί means 'after'. When once the Dawn has climbed up into the sky, the Sun-god has no respite; but during the night he has some rest, as the poet goes on to explain. This charming story was invented to account for the reappearance of the sun in the east after it had disappeared in the west.

5. τόν is the Sun-god.

6. ἐληλαμένη: In Greek when you fashion something out of metal you drive the metal; in Latin you lead it (cf. 'ductile' in English).

7. ἄκρον ἐφ᾽ ὕδωρ: 'over the top of the water'.

8, 9. The Hesperides lived in the far west, the Aethiopians in the far east.

9. ἵνα: 'where'.

10. ἑστᾶσι: 'are standing'.

11. ἐπεβήσετο: epic second aorist middle of ἐπιβαίνω.

SOLON, the Athenian statesman (c. 640–560 B.C.), was esteemed by the ancients as a very wise man, and one of the Seven Sages. As a poet he lacks the fine ear and felicity of Mimnermus; but his poems and the anecdotes told of him reveal a man of reflective mind and considerable intellectual scope, and highly civilized and graceful in his conversation.

1. This is a somewhat discursive poem, a sort of essay in verse. The poet follows the course of his thoughts from one topic to another. He begins with a prayer to the Muses (lines 1–8).

3. πρός with the genitive refers to the source from which something comes; ὄλβον πρὸς θεῶν is 'prosperity from the gods', and πρὸς ἀνθρώπων δόξαν ἔχειν ἀγαθήν is 'to have a good reputation proceeding from men'.

5. εἶναι depends on δότε (line 3). To be a joy to one's friends and a grief to one's enemies was considered highly desirable by the early Greeks. Your prosperity in itself gave grief to your enemies — in the *Odyssey* Odysseus says to Nausicaa that when a husband and wife live together in concord, it brings joy to their friends and grief to their enemies. (*Odyssey* 6, 182–5). — ὧδε is explained by line 6.

6. ἰδεῖν is an 'epexegetic' infinitive, limiting αἰδοῖον and δεινόν.

7. πεπᾶσθαι (from πάομαι): 'to have acquired', hence 'to possess'.

8. πάντως ἦλθε: 'is sure to come'. Gnomic aorist.

9–32. He has just said he doesn't desire wealth if he must get it unjustly; now follows an exposition of what happens to those who do.

9. πλοῦτον, which in its own clause should be nominative, is 'inversely' attracted to the case of its relative pronoun ὄν in the dependent clause.

10. νεάτου: irregular superlative of νέος, like μέσατος from μέσος. Here it means 'lowest'.

11. ὃν δέ is parallel to ὃν μέν in line 9. — ὑφ': 'under the influence of'.

11–13. The subject of ἔρχεται and ἔπεται is πλοῦτος. Wealth which is persuaded by unjust actions to come comes reluctantly and shamefully (οὐ κατὰ κόσμον). In line 11 wealth is pursued; in line 13 it follows.

13. ἀναμίσγεται: 'is found mingled with it'.

14. ἀρχή: sc. ἄτης.

16. οὐ δήν: 'not for long'.

17–25. The vengeance of Zeus is like a storm in spring; it breaks suddenly, and when it comes it makes a clean sweep, clearing the air.

18. ὥς τε: 'just as'.

21. ἔργα: 'tilled fields', the 'works' of the farmer.

25. τοιαύτη Ζηνὸς πέλεται τίσις: an anacoluthon, since strict grammar would require a verb to resume ἐξαπίνης δέ in line 17; but the sense is clear.

25ff. Zeus strikes sometimes soon, sometimes late, and like Jehovah he even visits the fathers' iniquities upon the children.

27. αἰεὶ διαμπερές: 'forever and ever'. — ἕ: Zeus. — λέληθε: gnomic perfect. The subject is ὅστις ἀλιτρὸν θυμὸν ἔχῃ.

28. ἐξεφάνη: 'he is found out'.

29. ἔτεισεν: aorist of τίνω, 'he makes requital', 'he pays'.

30. In Greek you can't say, "But those who themselves escape and whom the punishment of the gods doesn't strike", changing the case of the relative pronoun; you have to say, "But those who themselves escape (and the punishment of the gods doesn't strike them)".

31. The subject of ἤλυθε is μοῖρα. — αὖτις: 'hereafter'.

33–42. The point has been made that Zeus' vengeance is certain — the wicked man hopes to get away with his evil deeds, but he never does. Now the poet goes on to say that not only the wicked, but everyone alike (ὁμῶς ἀγαθός τε κακός τε) is deluded, and we all cheat ourselves with false opinions and false expectations.

34. εὖ: reflexive. — δεινός means 'terrible, wonderful', and frequently, as here, is used somewhat ironically: 'a frightfully good opinion of himself'.

35. τούτου: viz. παθεῖν τι.

37. χὦστις: crasis for καὶ ὅστις. — πιέσθη is from πιέζω.

38. 'lets his mind dwell on how he is going to recover.' ὡς ὑγιὴς ἔσται is simply indirect discourse; he merely expects to recover, he doesn't consider ways and means to recover.

40. καλός: supply ἄλλος δοκεῖ ἔμμεναι ἀνήρ.

43-70. He has just remarked that the poor man expects to get rich. This particular delusion he discusses at greater length than the others. Men, he says, optimistically pursue various callings in the hope of making money, but sometimes with good results and sometimes with bad, as the gods determine. There is risk in everything (πᾶσι δέ τοι κίνδυνος ἐπ' ἔργμασιν, line 65).

43. σπεύδει δ' ἄλλοθεν ἄλλος: supply κτήσασθαι χρήματα. 'One man tries to make money from one source, another from another'.

45. ἰχθυόεντ' apparently goes with πόντον in line 43.

47. Take πολυδένδρεον with γῆν. — εἰς ἐνιαυτόν: 'year in, year out'.

48. τοῖσιν: demonstrative used for relative.

51. ἄλλος: supply ξυλλέγεται βίοτον from line 50. — πάρα is so accentuated because it follows its object.

52. σοφίης is 'skill in song'.

56. ῥύσεται: 'fend off', 'avert'.

57. Παιῶνος: Paeon, the Homeric physician of the gods.

58. τέλος: 'sure achievement'.

62. Supply ἰητρός as subject of τίθησι, 'makes'.

64. δῶρα: the gifts of the gods were by no means always good.

66. σχήσειν: the nautical use, 'put to shore'. — χρήματος ἀρχομένου is genitive absolute.

67. Join οὐ προνοήσας to ἔπεσεν.

70. ἔκλυσιν ἀφροσύνης: 'a redemption from his folly'.

71–76. The poem closes with a few sombre apophthegms: there is no limit to human greed, which results in the punishment now of one man, now of another.

71. πεφασμένον (from φαίνω): 'revealed', 'stated', 'fixed'.

72. βιόν: 'substance', 'property'.

2. From the elegy called *Salamis*, which Solon wrote to spur the Athenians to complete the conquest of Salamis.

2. κόσμον ἐπέων: 'embellishment of words', i.e., 'in an ornamental style'; in apposition with ᾠδήν. —ἀντ᾽ ἀγορῆς: 'instead of an oration'. — θέμενος: 'having made for myself'.

3. εἴην: a future wish. — τότε: when we abandon Salamis. — Φολεγάνδριος: Pholegandrus and Sicinus were small and unimportant islands in the Aegean.

5. γένοιτο: potential optative.

6. τῶν Σαλαμιναφετῶν: 'of those who abandoned Salamis'.

7. ἴομεν: the Homeric short-vowel subjunctive of εἶμι. — μαχησόμενοι: future participle of purpose.

8. ἀπωσόμενοι: from ἀπωθέω.

3. The bad political situation at Athens.

1–2. κατά governs αἶσαν and φρένας.

5. αὐτοί: emphatic; 'the citizens themselves . . .'

7. οἶσιν ἑτοῖμον κτλ.: 'for whom it is prepared that they shall suffer much woe . . .'

8. ἐκ: 'as a consequence of'.

9. κόρος is 'having more than is good for you', and also the resulting insolence. Here, 'insolence'.

9–10. 'nor to observe good order in their present jubilation by feasting in quiet'.

16. ἦλθ᾽ ἀποτεισομένη: 'comes to exact the penalty'. The active means 'to pay'; the passive, 'to be paid off', hence 'to exact vengeance'.

17. πάσῃ πόλει: 'to the whole city', not merely to the guilty.
The ἕλκος is political disintegration and civil war.

19. στάσιν ἔμφυλον is civil discord; πόλεμον is foreign war.
A city torn by civil strife is an easy prey to its enemies.

20. ἡλικίην: 'youth'.

21. ἐκ: 'at the hands of' its enemies.

22. The sense of ἐν συνόδοις κτλ. is a trifle obscure.

25. πραθέντες: from πιπράσκω. Poor men are obliged to sell
themselves into slavery abroad.

26–29. The public distress comes home to everyone's house;
the front door won't keep it out any longer; it leaps over the
high wall of the courtyard, and finds out even those that hide
in the bedchamber.

27. ἔχειν: intransitive, 'to hold fast'.

29. εἰ καί: 'even if'.

30–40. The advantages of εὐνομίη over δυσνομίη.

35. ἄτη blossoms with an evil luxuriance.

4. 1. ἀγαθός is 'noble', κακός 'base'. A well-born man in
early Greece, if he was courageous and honest and generally
speaking a good representative of his class, was felt to have
ἀρετή, or excellence as a human being, which a man of low birth
could not aspire to. This poem reflects the confusion which
arose when some of the κακοί, in consequence of the commer-
cial revolution of the seventh century, became wealthy. The
older aristocrats (ἡμεῖς in this poem) felt that however wealthy
these *nouveaux riches* might be, they didn't have ἀρετή.

2. διαμείβομαι means 'receive in exchange'. That which you
receive is in the accusative; the price you pay is in the genitive.

3. τὸ μέν is ἀρετή.

4. Take ἀνθρώπων with ἄλλος.

5. This poem sets forth Solon's moderate political policy.

2. τιμῆς: partitive genitive. — ἐπορεξάμενος: 'offering yet
more'.

4. ἐφρασάμην: 'I took heed'.

8. ἀνεθείς: from ἀνίημι, 'allowed to run free'.

9. The geneaology of sin: πλοῦτος begets κόρος which begets ὕβρις which begets ἄτη.

11. Take πᾶσιν with ἀδεῖν.

10. 3. μονάρχου depends on δουλοσύνην.

5. With ἐξάραντα supply ἑαυτόν, 'when he has raised himself up'.

13. 1. ᾧ: dative of possessor.

19. The ten ages of man.

1. ἄνηβος: 'beardless'.

1-2. ἕρκος ὀδόντων φύσας ἐκβάλλει: 'having grown a fence of teeth sheds it'.

2. ἐν ἑπτ' ἔτεσιν: 'within seven years'.

4. ἥβης: 'puberty'.

5. With τριτάτῃ supply ἑβδομάδι, 'in the third period of seven years'.

8. ἰσχύν: accusative of limitation.

9. With ὥριον supply ἐστί.

10. παίδων γενεήν: 'an offspring consisting of children'.

13-14. ἑπτά and ὀκτώ are cardinal numbers somewhat awkwardly doing duty for ordinals.

15. δύναται: 'he retains his powers'.

22. A reply to fragment 6 of Mimnermus. Mimnermus had said that he hoped to be spared sickness and heavy cares, and to die in his sixtieth year.

1. 'Αλλ' εἴ μοι κἂν νῦν ἔτι πείσεαι: 'But if you will still be persuaded by me, even now . . .' καί strengthens νῦν. πείσεαι is subjunctive, as though in the protasis of a 'more vivid' future condition. Solon begs Mimnermus to change his poem, even though it's already finished. — ἔξελε (from ἐξαιρέω): 'remove'. — τοῦτον: sc. τὸν λόγον.

2. μεγαίρω is related to μέγας and means 'to think something too much for someone', hence 'to begrudge it him'.

3. μεταποίησον: μετά in compounds sometimes carries the idea of change. — Λιγυαστάδη: a title which Solon gives to Mimnermus; perhaps 'clear singer' renders it; it seems at least to be connected with λιγύς, 'clear'.

7. Take αἰεί, 'continually', with διδασκόμενος.

XENOPHANES was born at Colophon in 565 B.C.; and died, at a very advanced age, sometime after 473 B.C. When Colophon was taken by the Medes in 540, Xenophanes was obliged to flee; and thereafter he led a wandering life of which few details are known. He was one of the most audacious thinkers of his time. Like Thales and some other Ionian philosophers, he speculated on the nature of the physical universe. But his most original idea was his criticism of anthropomorphic religion, upon two grounds, first, that the poets had attributed conduct to the gods which in men would be held disgraceful; and secondly, that anthropomorphic gods are evidently creations of human fancy, since the gods of every people are like the people themselves.

1. A well-conducted symposium.

1. ζάπεδον = δάπεδον, 'floor'.

2. ἀμφιτιθεῖ: Ionic for ἀμφιτίθησι. Supply παῖς τις, the missing subject.

4. μεστὸς εὐφροσύνης: 'full of good cheer'.

5. ἄλλος: 'more'. — προδώσειν: 'fail'.

6. ἄνθεος ὀζόμενος: the crust which forms on old wines was called ἄνθος. ὄζω takes the genitive (perhaps partitive).

9. γεραρή: 'stately'.

10. τυροῦ: Verbs signifying fulness and want take the genitive of material. — ἀχθομένη: 'burdened'.

11. ἂν τὸ μέσον gives the position of the altar. (The MS text is corrupt in this place; and ἂν τὸ μέσον is not a very satisfactory job of mending it.) ἂν is for ἀνά.

13ff. Now that he has described the preparations, Xenopha-

nes lays down laws to govern the conduct of the entertainment
itself. First a hymn was sung by the whole company; then
followed a libation and prayer; then a round of songs sung by
individuals.

13. εὔφρονας: 'merry'.

15. The sequence is εὐξαμένους δύνασθαι πρήσσειν τὰ δίκαια.

15–17. σπείσαντας and εὐξαμένους are subjects of πίνειν
(line 17).

16. ὦν: Ionic for οὖν. — προχειρότερον: πρόχειρος usually
means 'at hand'. Here the duty of making a libation and prayer
is more 'at hand' than drinking.

17. ὁπόσον κεν ἔχων ἀφίκοιο: 'as much as you can hold and
reach home'. ἔχων is the conditional participle.

18. μὴ πάνυ γηραλέος: 'unless you're quite old'. Then you're
entitled to the help of a slave.

19. αἰνεῖν depends on χρή, (line 13). — ἐσθλά is the object
of ἀναφαίνῃ, not of πιών.

20. ὥς κτλ. explains ἐσθλά in line 19. — οἱ: dative of possessor. — τόνος ἀμφ' ἀρετῆς: 'a straining (or striving) after
virtue'.

21. διέπειν depends on χρή (line 13).

22. τῶν προτέρων: 'of the men of former times'. Xenophanes
doesn't think very highly of them.

23. στάσιας: accusative plural of στάσις. There was a fashion
of singing songs of political controversy at symposia. Xenophanes is against all mention of strife, whether among gods or men.

24. προμηθείην: 'reverence'. (Noun).

One suspects that a party of this sort would be more edifying
than entertaining.

2. Xenophanes asserts his claim to public honor against that
of the Olympic victors.

1. ἄροιτο is the epic second aorist of αἴρω, 'win'.

2. πενταθλεύων: the πένταθλον consisted of five events, the
broad-jump, the discus, the footrace, the wrestling-bout, and the
javelin-throw.

3. Πίσαο: genitive of Πίσης, a stream which flows into the Alpheus near Olympia.

4. ἔχων: ἔχω can mean 'have an understanding of'.

5. The pancration combined wrestling and boxing. — ἄεθλον can mean either a contest or a prize; here clearly it means the contest.

6. προσορᾶν is limiting infinitive with κυδρότερος: 'more illustrious to look upon'.

7. προεδρίην: the ringside seat, a privilege otherwise accorded only to high officials and to benefactors of the state.

8. σῖτα is the plural of σῖτος. 'Food at the public expense' is the right to take part in the free feasting at the Prytaneum, which was reserved for distinguished citizens.

9. κειμήλιον (cf. κεῖμαι): a 'nest-egg'. These were the marks of distinction which the state paid to the Olympic victor. In addition he would be received on his return home from Olympia with an elaborate hymn sung and danced by a chorus; and there are two examples of men who were accorded semi-divine honors because of their victories in the games, one of them while he was still alive. Pindar says, (*Olympian* I, 97–9)

ὁ νικῶν δὲ λοιπὸν ἀμφὶ βίοτον
ἔχει μελιτόεσσαν εὐδίαν
ἀέθλων ἕνεκεν.

'The victor all the rest of his life breathes a delicious and serene air because of his victory.' And Solon mentioned Cleobis and Bito of Argos as being among the happiest men of whom he had ever heard, because they had the good fortune to die on the day of their return from the games, while the citizens were celebrating their victory, and so experienced no anti-climax. Such was the halo of the athletic victor, of which Xenophanes here expresses his envy.

10. With ἵπποισιν supply νίκην ἄροιτο.

11. οὐκ ἐὼν ἄξιος ὥσπερ ἐγώ: 'though he is not so worthy of these rewards as I'.

12. ἠδ' ἵππων: fine indignant scorn in that ἵππων. — By σοφίη Xenophanes probably means (1) wisdom, and (2) the ability to put it in verse.

13. εἰκῇ: 'thoughtlessly'. — τοῦτο νομίζεται: 'this opinion is held' — namely that ῥώμη is more valuable than σοφίη. Or perhaps, 'this custom prevails'.

15. ἀγαθός agrees with πύκτης to be sure, 'a good boxer'; but it must also be understood as introducing πενταθλεῖν (limiting infinitive), 'good at the pentathlon', as well as παλαισμοσύνην (limiting accusative), 'good at wrestling', and ταχυτῆτι ποδῶν (causal dative), 'good on account of his swiftness of foot'.

17. τόπερ: the demonstrative instead of the relative. — πρότιμον: the footrace was the oldest event at the Olympic games, and therefore πρότιμος, though in the fifth century a victory in the chariot race was most highly esteemed.

18. Take ῥώμης with ἔργα; ἀνδρῶν probably goes best with ῥώμης, 'deeds of men's strength', though it could be taken with ἔργα or even with ἀγῶνι.

20. ἐπὶ τῷ: 'on account of this:'. τῷ is explained by line 21.

22. μυχούς: 'treasure chambers'.

10. 1. ἀνέθηκαν: 'ascribed'.

12. 1. This line is an iambic trimeter (see page 73). — δοκέουσι γεννᾶσθαι θεούς: '. . . suppose that the gods are begotten'.

13. "If cattle and horses could draw . . ."
1–5. A condition contrary to fact.

2. γράψαι: 'to paint' or 'to draw'. — ἔργα τελεῖν: 'make sculptures'.

4. ἰδέας: 'forms' drawn or painted. — σώματα: 'bodies', sculptured.

5. οἷόν περ δέμας is somewhat untranslatably made correlative with τοιαῦτα σώματα: 'such shape as they have themselves, that kind of bodies they would make for (lit. of) the gods too'.

14. An early example of cultural relativism.

16. 2. The subject of ἐφευρίσκουσιν is θνητοί.

18. Being comfortable by the fire, and talking over old times.

3. ὑποτρώγωντ' ἐρεβίνθους: 'munching chickpeas'.

5. ὁ Μῆδος: Harpagus, who took Colophon.

20. 'He is all eye, all mind, all ear.' — οὖλος = ὅλος, 'entire'. 'He' is the universe.

30. 2. ἄσσα: Ionic for ἅτινα.

3. εἰ καί: 'even if'.

4. ὅμως: 'nevertheless'. — τέτυκται: perfect passive of τεύχω. δόκος is 'mere opinion', 'fancy'.

THEOGNIS of Megara was a poor but disdainful aristocrat who lived in the sixth century B.C., in a time of revolution and civil war. He had had lands and lost them, and was obliged to go into exile. He wrote a great many short elegiac poems which he addressed to his young friend Cyrnus; some of these give worldly advice, others are simply an expression of his opinions on politics, society, and personal relationships.

27. ὑποθήσομαι: 'instruct'.

28. ἀπὸ τῶν ἀγαθῶν: Theognis believed that virtue was learned by association with aristocrats, and that nothing was so profitable to a young man as keeping good company, nor anything so disastrous as association with the κακοί.

30. ἕλκεο: 'draw to yourself', 'amass'.

32. ἔχεο: 'cleave to'.

53-58. Times have changed: men who before were serfs have become citizens and advanced to honor, while men who were once noble are no longer regarded.

55. κατέτριβον: 'wore to tatters'.

56. ἐνέμοντο: 'grazed'. These men are no better than brutes.

57. ἀγαθοί: sarcastic. — Πολυπαΐδη: 'son of Polypaus', Cyrnus.

69. πίσυνος: 'with confidence'; an adjective agreeing with the subject, where we would use an adverb.

70. σπουδαῖον: 'serious'.

71. πολλὰ μογήσας is concessive: 'even though it cost much labor'.

77. ἀντερύσασθαι: 'to be valued equally with'. — χρυσοῦ is genitive of price.

78. ἄξιος: supply ἐστί. — διχοστασίη: 'quarrel', perhaps private, perhaps political.

87–92. Against duplicity.

87. στέργε: 'love'. — ἄλλῃ: 'elsewhere'.

91. δίχ᾽ ἔχει νόον: 'has a divided mind'.

92. With ἐχθρός supply ὤν; with βέλτερος supply ἐστί.

173. Join μάλιστα πάντων: 'most of all things'.

174. 'more than old age or a fever'. The genitives γήρως and ἠπιάλου may be explained as genitives of comparison, the idea of comparison proceeding from μάλιστα; or as particular illustrations of πάντων.

178. γλῶσσα δὲ οἱ δέδεται: to which Bion replied, "How then can you, who say you are a poor man, talk so much nonsense and weary us so with your chatter?"

183–92. In which we learn that marriage is only another kind of stock-breeding.

184. εὐγενέας: 'thoroughbreds'. — ἐξ ἀγαθῶν: 'from good sires'.

185. κτήσασθαι: supply κριούς, etc. — κακὴν κακοῦ: 'the low-born daughter of a low-born father'.

188. ἀφνεόν: supply ἄνδρα. — βούλεται: supply γῆμαι.

190. πλοῦτος ἔμειξε γένος: 'money confounds breed'.

192. σύν is adverbial.

209–10. The friendlessness of exile.

209. φεύγοντι: 'the exile'.

210. φυγῆς: 'exile'. Genitive of comparison.

213–18. Imitate the action of the polyp — be all things to all men.

213. ποικίλον: 'changeable'.

214. ὀργήν: 'temper', 'disposition'.

215. πολυπλόκου: 'tangled', that is, 'with writhing tentacles'. The polyp appears to change color with its surroundings, like the chameleon.

216. τῇ: demonstrative for relative. — προσομιλήσῃ (aorist subjunctive): 'cling to'. — ἰδεῖν: limiting infinitive, 'in appearance'.

217. τῇδ': 'in this direction'. — χρόα (accusative of limitation): 'in complexion'. (He returns to the metaphor of the polyp.)

218. ἀτροπίης: 'unadaptability'.

363. εὖ κώτιλλε: 'speak fair'. — ὑποχείριος: 'under your hand', that is, 'in your power'. — τεῖσαι is the aorist infinitive of τίνω: 'pay him back'.

393–8. The good man is stoical in poverty.

395. τοῦ is explained by οὗ τέ περ κτλ.

397. οὔτε κακοῖσ' ἕπεται νόος οὔτ' ἀγαθοῖσιν: 'his mind accommodates itself neither to good fortune nor to bad'. In good fortune the bad man is arrogant, in bad fortune abject.

398. τά τε καὶ τά: κακά and ἀγαθά.

527. ἥβης: exclamatory genitive.

528. ἀπονισσομένης: 'going away'.

533. ὑπό: 'to the accompaniment of'.

534. ὀχέων = ἔχων.

605. λιμοῦ: genitive of comparison.

847–850. The poet expresses his scorn for the people by giving this contemptuous advice to the demagogue.

847. ἐπίβα: imperative, for ἐπίβηθι.

849. φιλοδέσποτον: 'loving their master'. Elsewhere this word is used only of slaves and dogs.

983. 'Let us surrender our hearts to feasting'.

984. τερπωλῆς: partitive genitive, 'some pleasure'.

1197–1200. The poet is reminded of his lost home.

1197. ὄρνιθος: the crane.

1199. ὡραίον: 'timely'.

237–254. Envoi and reproach.

238. πωτήσει: from πωτάομαι, an epic variant of πέτομαι. — γῆν as well as πόντον is governed by ἐπί. Cyrnus will fly over the sea and land, because wherever in Greece there is feasting, he will be present and will live on the lips of the singers.

240. ἐν πάσαις goes with θοίνῃς and εἰλαπίνῃσι.

241. An αὐλίσκος is a little flute. At symposia elegies were sung to the accompaniment of the flute.

241–3. καί σε . . . καλά τε καὶ λιγέα ᾄσονται: 'and they will sing your praises sweet and clear'. ἀείδω, 'celebrate', takes an accusative of the person celebrated; and also quite without difficulty, another accusative limiting the quality of the song. The central idea of the accusative is *limitation*, and you can limit as much as you please.

245. οὐδὲ θανών: 'not even when you are dead'. οὐδέ is the opposite of καί.

245–6. μελήσεις ἀνθρώποισι: 'you will be a concern to men'.

246. Take ἄφθιτον with ὄνομα, and αἰέν with ἄφθιτον.

251. ὅσοισι μέμηλε: supply ταῦτα (viz. the gifts of the Muses). — καὶ ἐσσομένοισιν: 'even to those who shall live hereafter'. Cf. *Odyssey* 8, 580: ἵνα ᾖσι καὶ ἐσσομένοισιν ἀοιδή.

252. ὁμῶς: 'alike', 'equally' (but ὅμως, 'nevertheless').

253–4. Cyrnus, it appears, was sometimes disrespectful. Cf. lines 1103–4:

> ὕβρις καὶ Μάγνητας ἀπώλεσε καὶ Κολοφῶνα
> καὶ Σμύρνην πάντως, Κύρνε, καὶ ὕμμ' ἀπολεῖ.

253. αἰδοῦς: partitive genitive with τυγχάνω.

ARCHILOCHUS of Paros flourished in the first half of the 7th century B.C. He was a soldier of fortune, and he lived a rough life full of hardships and disappointments. He was a man of violent passions; his spleen was proverbial in antiquity, and his poems were held up as models of trenchant hate. These to be sure have mostly not survived; from those which have, we should infer rather a resilient, courageous personality capable of delicate nuances of feeling, more often wistful or poignant than ferocious. He is one of the creative pioneers in Greek versification: he first perfected iambic and trochaic verse as a literary medium; and if he lived as early as recent investigators believe, he was the first master of elegy also.

1. 1. Ἐνναλίοιο: a title of the war-god, Ares.

2. 1. μᾶζα: 'barley cake'. — μεμαγμένη: from μάσσω, 'knead'.

2. Ἰσμαρικός: Ismarus was on the coast of Thrace; Archilochus at one time campaigned in Thrace.

3. 1. ἐπί is adverbial. — θαμειαί: 'thick', that is, much in evidence.

2. μῶλον: the moil of war.

4. αἴμονες = δαήμονες, 'skilful'. — ταύτης μάχης: 'in this type of warfare'.

5. Εὐβοίης: Euboea, somewhat before or after 700, was shaken by the Lelantine War between Chalcis and Eretria. Archilochus appears to have been on the scene of these hostilities too, and may have taken part in them.

6. 1. Σαΐων: the Saii lived near Abdera in Thrace.

2. ἔντος: 'weapon'. This word appears elsewhere only in the plural.

4. ἐρρέτω: from ἔρρω, which is a colloquial word. 'To hell with that shield!' — κακίω: accusative of κακίων, 'worse'.

7. 1. κήδεα: object of μεμφόμενος.

3. τοίους: 'those men' for whom Pericles and the city grieve; but with the implication that they were good men. —κατά is adverbial; κῦμα is the subject.

4. ἔκλυσεν: aorist of κλύζω, 'overwhelmed'. — οἰδαλέους: 'swollen'.

6. ἐπί: adverbial, with ἔθεσαν, 'have established'. —τλημο-
σύνην: in apposition with φάρμακον.

7. τάδε: griefs.

9. ἐπαμείψεται: 'pass over to'.

18. In iambic trimeter. Archilochus used this metre for
satiric verse; later it became established as the metre of the
spoken verses of Attic drama. The verse consists of three double
iambs:

$$\cup - \cup - \mid \cup - \cup - \mid \cup - \cup -.$$

Ordinarily there is a clearly-felt division of the line into slightly
unequal halves; either

$$\cup - \cup - \mid \cup \quad - \cup - \mid \cup - \cup -; \text{ or}$$
$$\cup - \cup - \mid \cup - \cup \quad - \mid \cup - \cup -;$$

this division is called the *caesura*. It very seldom falls in the
exact centre of the line. The first syllable of a double iamb
(but not the third syllable) may be long instead of short. That
is, a double iamb may have the pattern $- - \cup -$, but not
$\cup - - -$. Any long syllable in the first two double iambs may
be 'resolved' into two short syllables. (For example, line 4 of
this fragment is scanned,

$$- \quad \cup\cup \quad \cup \quad - \mid \cup \qquad \| \qquad - \quad \cup \quad - \mid \cup - \quad \cup -$$

οὐδ' ἔρα- τος οἶ - ος ‖ ἀμ - φὶ Σί - ριος ῥοάς

In the first double iamb, the first syllable is long instead of
short, and the second syllable, which should be long, is resolved
into two shorts. The caesura falls early in the second double-
iamb.)

1. ἥδε: the island of Thasos, which Archilochus helped to
colonize. — ῥάχις: 'backbone'.

2. ἐπιστεφής: 'crowned with'. — ὕλης is genitive of material
after a word expressing fulness or emptiness.

3. τι: 'by any means'.

4. The Siris: a nice river. (Where it was is a matter of con-
jecture.)

22. 1. Γύγεω: Gyges was a rich king of Lydia who reigned early in the 7th century B.C.

2. ἀγαίομαι = ἄγαμαι, 'envy'.

3. ἐρέω is Ionic for ἐράω. — τυραννίδος (a 'partitive' genitive): 'monarchy'. The first appearance of this word in Greek.

25. Vignette of a young girl.

1. θαλλόν: 'twig'.

2. ῥοδῆς: 'rose-bush'.

53. A regretful line.

The metre is trochaic tetrameter catalectic, which consists of four double trochees:

$$- \cup - \cup \quad - \cup - \cup \quad - \cup - \cup \quad - \cup -,$$

of which the last is incomplete. This line is always divided after the second double trochee. The fourth syllable of a double trochee may be long, but not the second syllable: $- \cup - -$, but not $- - \cup -$. A long syllable may be resolved into two short ones.

54. The colonization of Thasos didn't proceed smoothly. There was trouble with the neighboring barbarians of Thrace, in addition to the discouragement afforded by the island itself.

58. 1. τίθει: 'attribute'.

3. εὖ βεβηκότας: 'well established'. The perfect of βαίνω means 'be situated'.

5. χρήμη: 'in want'. — νόον παρήορος: An extra horse (called the ἵππος παρήορος) was sometimes harnessed to pull alongside the regular team; since he was apt to be friskier than the others, the word παρήορος came to mean 'wild' or 'distraught', which is its meaning here. νόου is a genitive of separation ('reft of sense').

60. The marks of a good general.

1. διαπεπλιγμένον: 'swaggering', from διαπλίσσομαι.

2. γαῦρον: 'exulting in'.

3. ἰδεῖν: limiting infinitive with ῥοικός, 'bow-legged'.

67. 1. κυκώμενε (from κυκάω): 'stirred up', 'disturbed'.

2. ἀνάδυ: second aorist imperative of ἀναδύομαι, 'rise up'. His θυμός, which a moment ago was a troubled body of water, is now to rise up from the waves. — δυσμενῶν depends on ἐναντίον.

4. ἀσφαλέως: 'stedfastly'. — ἀμφάδην: 'openly', (related to φαίνω).

7. γίγνωσκε: 'recognize'. — ῥυσμός (Ionic for ῥυθμός) means 'measured motion'; here apparently the alternation between prosperity and adversity. — ἔχει: 'governs'.

71. Archilochus loved a girl named Neobule, and hoped to marry her, since she had been promised to him by her father Lycambes. When Lycambes broke his promise Archilochus took it very hard, and attacked both father and daughter with such savage satire that they are reported to have hanged themselves.

1. εἰ γάρ: introducing a wish. — ὥς: 'thus', illustrating with a gesture, as often in Greek.

74. The consternation caused by an eclipse of the sun, perhaps that of April 6th, 648 B.C., but more probably that of March 14th, 711.

1. ἀπώμοτον: Something is ἀπώμοτον if you can take an oath that it's impossible or untrue.

5. ἐκ τοῦ: understand χρόνου, 'from now on'. — πιστὰ πάντα καὶ ἐπίελπτα: πάντα is the subject. 'Anything can be expected now'. πιστά, 'credible'.

7. μηδέ: 'not even'. — θῆρες are land-beasts; they receive in exchange (ἀνταμείψωνται) a sea pasture (νομὸν ἐνάλιον) at the expense of the dolphins (δελφῖσι). δελφῖσι is explained, not without strain, as a dative of disadvantage; though we need not assume that the dolphins get the worst of the bargain, since in line 9 we learn that they may be expected to like the mountain.

8. σφιν refers to the land-beasts still.

9. τοῖσι: these are the dolphins.

77. This is the first mention of the dithyramb, or choral dance in honor of Dionysus, from which Attic tragedy arose.

1. ἐξάρξαι: 'to lead off'.

2. You can't do it sober.

88. A sample of Archilochus' satire against Lycambes. Lycambes must have been uncommonly thin-skinned if he succumbed to such shafts as these. — This poem is in a stanza called the *epode*, which consists of an iambic trimeter followed by an iambic dimeter (two double iambs).

2. παρήειρε is from παραείρω, 'distort'.

3. ἠρήεισθα: pluperfect of ἀραρίσκω: 'those wits with which you were fitted (or equipped) before'.

89–94. Fragments of the fable of the Fox and the Eagle. The fox and the eagle go into partnership. The eagle treacherously robs the fox of her young, and feeds them to the little eaglets. When the fox discovers her loss, she is mocked by the eagle, and prays to Zeus to avenge her. The eagle, going too far, robs some sacrificial meat from an altar. Live coals clinging to the meat set his nest afire, the eaglets fall out, and the fox eats them.

89. 1. αἶνος: 'fable'.

2. ἄρα: not interrogative, but asseverative. — καιετός = καὶ αἰετός. — ξυνωνίην = κοινωνίαν, 'partnership'.

3. ἔμειξαν: from μίγνυμι.

90. The fox's young are fed to the eaglets.

1. αἰηνές: 'dreadful', 'grievous'.

92. The eagle mocks the fox.

1. ἵνα: 'where'.

2. παλίγκοτος: 'forbidding'.

3. τῷ is demonstrative. — σὴν ἐλαφρίζων μάχην: 'making light of your hostility'.

4–6. He invites the fox to fly up and take revenge.

4. κυκλῶσαι: infinitive used for imperative.
6. ἀρθεῖσαν: from αἴρω.

94. The fox's prayer.
2. ἐπί: adverb with ὁρᾷς.
3. λεωργά: 'knavish'.

HIPPONAX. This poem is in choliambic metre, which is the same as iambic trimeter, except that in the last double iamb the third syllable is always long. This produces a limping effect which some of the satiric poets found effective.

LYRIC POETRY

The Greeks, when they spoke of a lyric poet, meant a poet who composed verses to be sung to the lyre. Elegy was sung to the flute, iambic verses were recited, and epic poetry, though accompanied by the lyre, was probably not sung but chanted. Of lyric poetry there were two types. One was choral poetry, which was sung and danced by a chorus, usually to express feelings which a group or even the whole community might share, and very often as an act of worship to a god, in celebration of some festival. In general the chorus would preserve a sort of dramatic anonymity, but at times it would quite freely become the mouthpiece of the poet himself, or even abandon its public character so far that individual dancers would recall their own personality and tease and joke with each other — there is a maiden's chorus by Alcman in which such a lapse of anonymity charmingly happens. The other type of lyric poetry was the monody or solo, which the poet accompanied himself, and in which he spoke directly, in his own person, to express his personal feelings.

ALCMAN lived in Sparta and wrote choral poetry there at some time (it is uncertain when) during the seventh century

B.C. There is a tradition that he was not born at Sparta, but came there as a slave from Sardis in Lydia. The Sparta of Alcman's time was not yet the barracks which it later became — music and the other arts were cultivated, and society was free and gay. Alcman's favorite form was the παρθενείον, or song for a chorus of maidens. His style is simple, animated, and charming.

58. The metre of this poem is a combination of trochaic and dactylic rhythms.

1–2. φάραγγες are clefts or watercourses; πρώονες are headlands, and χαράδραι are chasms. ὀρέων should be understood with all.

4. γένος μελισσᾶν: 'the race of bees'. μελισσᾶν is the Doric genitive plural.

94. He complains that he is too old to take part in the dance with his chorus of maidens, and wishes he were a kingfisher.

(Metre: dactylic hexameters, without substitution.)

1. παρθενικαί: 'maidens'.

2. βάλε introduces a wish: 'would that I were a kingfisher!' κηρύλος is the male kingfisher, and ἀλκύων the female. It is possible that his chorus was called Ἀλκύονες, 'Kingfishers'; there was one called 'Doves'.

3. κύματος ἄνθος: 'the crest of the wave'.

4. νηδεές: 'fearless'. — ἰαρός: Doric for ἱερός.

STESICHORUS of Himera (c. 630–555 B.C.) was a choral poet who flourished in Magna Graecia. He built his poems on an ample plan, launching upon extended narrative, and treating his mythical material not merely as example or illustration, but at length for its own sake. Very small fragments of his work survive.

6. From a poem about Heracles' search for the cattle of Geryon. Heracles is helped on his journey to the far west by the Sun-god, who has a golden cup (recall Mimnermus' "golden bed") in which he returns every night to the far east, where he rises in the morning. This cup the Sun-god lends to Heracles; and he, arriving at evening in the west, gives back the cup to the Sun-god.

(The metre is dactylic, except for the last line, which goes
$-\;-\;\cup\;\cup\;-\;\cup\;-\;|\;-\;\cup\;\cup\;-\;\cup\;-$. The 3rd, 4th and 5th lines each lead off with two short syllables; this introduction is called anacrusis or 'striking up'.)

1. Ἀέλιος: The choral poets affected the Doric dialect, whether it was native to them or not; even in the choruses of Attic tragedy there are many Doric forms. Doric very often has α for η, as here Ἀέλιος for Ἠέλιος, Ὑπεριονίδας for Ὑπεριονίδης, ἔβα for ἔβη.

10. From the marriage of Menelaus and Helen; they leave Helen's home to go in his chariot to Menelaus', and the by-standers throw flowers.

(The metre is dactylic; but the first line begins with a double trochee, $-\;\cup\;-\;\cup$.)

1. μᾶλα: 'quinces'. (Doric for μῆλα). — ποτερρίπτευν: ποτί = πρός. ἐρρίπτευν = ἐρρίπτον: there was a form ῥιπτέω as well as ῥίπτω.

3. οὔλας: 'twined', 'twisted'.

ALCAEUS was born about 620 B.C. at Mitylene on the island of Lesbos. Like Theognis, he was an aristocrat of the most narrow views. He passed a great part of his life in struggles with the successive tyrants of Mitylene, Myrsilus and Pittacus, who represented the new mercantile class. He was compelled at least twice to go into exile. His poems are monodies or solos, composed in the Aeolic dialect. Some were inspired by crises in the civil struggles in which he took part; others arose from oc-casions of private interest to the poet and his friends. Most of them are full of high spirits and conviviality; his repeated advice is, "Drink!"

2. An invocation to Hermes, in the Sapphic stanza,

$$- \cup - \overline{\cup} - \cup \cup - \cup - \cup$$
$$- \cup - \overline{\cup} - \cup \cup - \cup - \cup$$
$$- \cup - \overline{\cup} - \cup \cup - \cup - \cup$$
$$- \cup \cup - \cup$$

1. ὀ: The peculiarities of the Aeolic dialect are many and vexatious. One of them is *the complete absence of the rough breathing*. — μέδεις: present participle of μέδημι. *In Aeolic, most of the verbs which appear in other dialects as contract verbs are conjugated as* μι *verbs*. Now there was a form μεδέω as well as the more common μέδω, 'rule'; in Aeolic it appears as μέδημι; and its present participle is μέδεις, not μεδείς as it would be in any other dialect, because *accent in Aeolic is recessive*. — Κυλλάνας ὀ μέδεις, 'lord of Cyllene', means Hermes.

2. With θῦμος supply ἐστί. — ὕμνην: Aeolic for ὑμνεῖν. — τόν: relative. — κορύφαισιν: of Mount Olympus.

30. The battered Ship of State. The metre is the Alcaic stanza,

$$\overline{\cup} - \cup - \overline{\cup} - \cup \cup - \cup -$$
$$\overline{\cup} - \cup - \overline{\cup} - \cup \cup - \cup -$$
$$\overline{\cup} - \cup - \overline{\cup} - \cup - \cup$$
$$- \cup \cup - \cup \cup - \cup - \cup$$

1. ἀσυννέτημι: Aeolic for ἀσυννετέω. — στάσιν: 'dissension', the regular word for civil conflict.

2. ἔνθεν . . . ἔνθεν: 'from this side . . . from that'. Take τό with κῦμα.

3. ἄμμες is Aeolic for ἡμεῖς. — ὄν: this is what ἀνά looks like in Aeolic.

4. νᾶϊ: dative of ναῦς. *Aeolic, like Doric, has a predilection for ᾱ instead of η.* — φορήμεθα: from φόρημι = φορέω.

5. μόχθεντες: a present participle, from μόχθημι = μοχθέω.

6. πέρ is for περί: it is adverbial and should be taken with ἔχει, 'surrounds'.

7. πάν: Aeolic for πᾶν. — ζάδηλον is related to δηλέομαι. Translate 'torn to shreds'.

8. αὗτο: recessive accent.

9. χόλαισι: 3rd person plural of χόλαιμι, Attic χαλάω, 'give way'.

39. A great occasion, the death of the tyrant Myrsilus. (These are the first two lines of an Alcaic strophe.)

1. Understand τινα as subject of both infinitives, μεθύσθην and πώνην. *Aeolic infinitives regularly end in -ην.* — πὲρ βίαν: 'beyond his strength', 'more than he can hold'. πέρ is περί, having suffered apocope; but its sense is that of ὑπέρ.

2. πώνω is Aeolic for πίνω.

90. (Alcaic strophe.)

1. ὔει μὲν ὁ Ζεῦς: ὔει usually refers to rain; but here the context requires us to translate, 'Zeus sends a blizzard'. — ὀράνω: genitive singular of ὄρανος (= οὐρανός). *In Aeolic the genitive singular of the o-declension ends in ω.*

2. πεπάγαισιν (perfect, 3rd person plural, of πήγνυμι): 'are frozen'.

3. κάββαλε = κατάβαλλε, 'overthrow', 'strike down'.

4. ἐν is adverbial. — κέρναις: Aeolic aorist participle of κέρνημι, which is a poetic variant of κεράννυμι.

6. γνόφαλλον = κνέφαλλον, meaning apparently a fillet of wool.

91. (Alcaic strophe.)

1. θῦμον ἐπιτρέπην: 'to give over our hearts' to our troubles.

2. πρόκοψομεν οὐδέν: 'we shall get nowhere'.

3. ἀσάμενοι, 'by being vexed'. From ἄσαμι (= ἀσάω).

4. ἐνεικαμένοις: One of the most misleading peculiarities of Aeolic is that *the accusative plural of the vowel declension ends in -οις or -αις instead of -ους or -ᾱς*. (The *dative* plural always ends in -οισι or -αισι, except for the definite article, which is τοῖς or ταῖς). So ἐνεικαμένοις is the accusative plural of the first aorist middle participle of φέρω. The middle is causative; the accusative is in agreement with ἄμμε (= ἡμᾶς), which is the im-

plied subject of μεθύσθην. Translate 'the best remedy is for us to have wine brought and get drunk'.

50. To his brother Antimenidas, who had just returned from serving as a mercenary in the Babylonian army.

Metre: lesser Asclepiadean, which consists of a trochee, two choriambs, and an iamb,

$$- \cup - \cup \cup - - \cup \cup - \cup -;$$

but in this poem an iamb or a spondee may replace the introductory trochee.

2. λάβαν: Aeolic for λάβην, with ā for η, as frequently. — τῶ: genitive singular.

3. συμμάχεις: present participle from συμμάχημι, Aeolic for συμμαχέω.

5. κτένναις: present participle of κτέννω = κτείνω. — μαχαίταν = μαχήτην. — βασιληίων agrees with παχέων (line 7). The 'royal cubit' was 21 inches, so that this fighter, who lacked only one palm (four inches) of five royal cubits, was 8 feet 5 inches tall. He therefore surpassed Heracles, who measured 8 feet; but neither can be counted a real giant, since the traditional minimum height for giants was 5 royal cubits, or 8 feet 9 inches.

6. ἴαν: Lesbian Aeolic for μίαν.

7. παχέων = πήχεων. — ἀπύ is Aeolic for ἀπό. — πέμπων: genitive plural of πέμπε = πέντε, 'five', which elsewhere is indeclinable.

63. μελλιχόμειδε: Aeolic for μειλιχόμειδε. — Σάπφοι: vocative, 'Sappho'.

98. ἐπάιον (for ἐπήιον): imperfect of ἐπάιω, 'hear'. ἦρος is genitive after a verb of hearing.

2. τῶ μελιάδεος: understand οἴνω. (genitive singular).

(The metre of this poem is dactylic hexameter, but with a lame first foot.)

104. δίοπτρον: 'spyhole'; because a man reveals his true sentiments when he's drunk.

97. First things first. (Metre, greater Asclepiadean, which consists of a trochee, *three* choriambs, and an iamb.) — Take together μηδὲν ἄλλο δένδριον; ἀμπέλω is genitive of comparison, with πρότερον.

54. An inventory of armor. (Metre: each line consists of two glyconics plus a double iamb: $- \bar{\cup} \quad - \cup \cup - \cup -$ $- \bar{\cup} - \cup \cup - \cup - \quad \bar{\cup} - \cup -$.)

1. παῖσα: Aeolic for πᾶσα. — Ἄρῃ: dative of interest.

2. κυνίαισι is the instrumental dative. κυνία = κυνέη, 'helmet'. — κάτ: by apocope for κατά. — τᾶν is the Aeolic contraction of τάων, which in Attic becomes τῶν.

3. νεύοισιν: Aeolic for νεύουσιν. — πασσάλοις: *accusative* plural.

4. κρύπτοισιν: Aeolic for κρύπτουσιν. — περικείμεναι: περί in the lyric poets is often used instead for ὑπέρ. — ἄρκος: 'protection'. (ἄρκος is related to ἀρκέω). — ἰσχύρω: genitive singular, with βέλευς, which is a contraction of βέλεος.

5. νέω λίνω: genitive singular. — κοίιλαι is for κοῖλαι. — κατά is adverbial. — With βεβλήμεναι understand εἰσί: 'are lying' (on the floor).

6. πάρ is παρά; it is used adverbially. — σπάθαι are broadswords; and the κυπασσίς was a kind of chiton which reached to the middle of the thigh.

7. ὐπά is the Aeolic version of ὑπό, and should be taken together with ἔσταμεν, 'we have undertaken'.

SAPPHO, the most celebrated of women poets, was born on Lesbos about 610 B.C. Her family were aristocrats and suffered exile in the course of the civil broils of the end of the seventh century in Mitylene; they appear to have gone to Sicily, taking Sappho with them, but about 590 they were permitted to return, and Sappho spent the rest of her life in Mitylene. There she was the leader of a group of young girls, who formed around her an institution which was partly an academy of music and poetry, and partly a religious order, or θίασος, devoted to the cult of Aphrodite. Sappho at various times fell in love with several of these girls. At some time in her life she was married and had a daughter, whose name was Cleis. The date of her death is not known.

1. This poem is a lyric monody in the form of a prayer to Aphrodite, whom Sappho begs to help her to win her love. The prayer follows a canonical form: first an invocation to the goddess (lines 1–2); then the petition, followed by a reminder to the goddess of a former occasion on which she has helped Sappho (3–24); and finally a repetition of the plea to come to her assistance.

Metre, Sapphic stanza.

$$- \cup - \bar{\cup} - \cup \cup - \cup - \cup \quad \text{three times,}$$
$$- \cup \cup - \cup.$$

1. ποικιλόθρονε: 'having a richly-wrought throne'.

3. ὀνίαισι is Aeolic for ἀνίαις, 'troubles'. Aeolic occasionally has o for α. — δάμνα: as though imperative of δαμνάω, but probably a shortened form of δάμνᾱθι.

4. θῦμον: limiting accusative.

5. τυῖδε: Aeolic adverb, 'hither'. — αἴ ποτα = εἰ ποτε. — κἀτέρωτα = καὶ ἐτέρωτα, 'and at another time also'. ἐτέρωτα is an Aeolic adverb, used instead of ἄλλοτε. The *reminder* to the god could take two forms, either 'if ever I did anything for you, do this for me now', or as here, 'if ever you helped me before, help me now'.

6. αὔδως: genitive of αὔδω (Aeolic for αὐδή, 'voice'). — ἀίοισα: Aeolic for ἀίουσα, 'hearing'. — πήλυι: Aeolic adverb, 'from afar off'. The υι is a diphthong.

7. ἔκλυες: not simply 'you heard' but 'you heeded'.

8. Take χρύσιον with ἄρμα.

9. ὑπασδεύξαισα = ὑποζεύξουσα: Aeolic has σδ for ζ, and ὑπα- for ὑπο-.

10. στροῦθοι: 'sparrows'. — περί: for ὑπέρ.

11. δίννηντες: present participle of δίννημι (= δινέω), 'whirling', or 'fluttering'. πύκνα could mean 'downy'; but since the birds are sparrows, their wings might be 'numerous'. Many sparrows (I suppose) would be needed, if not for horsepower, then at all events for looks. — ὀρράνω: genitive singular, = οὐρανοῦ.

13. ἐξίκοντο: 'they arrived'. (ἐκ in compounds frequently conveys the idea of completion.)

14. Splendor and mystery are transformed by this fine line into a soft benignity.

15. ἤρεο: 'you asked', from ἠρόμην. — δηὖτε = δὴ αὖτε, 'now again'. — κὤττι is for καὶ ὄττι.

17. Take μοι with γένεσθαι, and μαινόλᾳ θύμῳ with θέλω, 'in my mad heart'. μαινόλᾳ is dative singular masculine, from μαινόλης which follows the ᾱ-declension.

18–24. Here the construction changes from indirect to direct discourse — the very words of the goddess.

18. Πείθω: Persuasion, who along with Eros was attendant on Aphrodite. Πείθω (accusative) should be taken as the subject, and τίνα as the object, of ἄγην.

19. μαῖσ' = μαῖσαι, second person singular from μαῖμαι = μάομαι, 'do you desire'. The whole clause may be translated, "Whom this time do you desire that Peitho should lead to love you?" — εἰς σὰν φιλότᾱτα: literally 'into love of you'. φιλότᾱτα is for φιλότητα.

20. Ψάπφα: vocative. — ἀδικήει = ἀδικεῖ: "Who wrongs you?"

21. καὶ γάρ: elliptical. Understand some such words as 'Be comforted', καὶ γὰρ κτλ.

22. "And if she refuses your gifts, nay but she will give gifts . . ." — δέκεται = δέχεται.

24. κωὖκ: for καὶ οὐκ. καί used in this way with the participle means 'even'.

25. Now, having reminded the goddess of this former inter-

cession, Sappho returns to her present need. — Understand με as the object of λῦσον.

26. μερίμναν is for μεριμνᾶν, genitive plural; the same applies to χαλέπαν in the line above. — Understand σε as the subject of τέλεσσαι.

27. ἰμέρρει: Aeolic for ἰμείρει.

28. ἔσσο: middle imperative of ἔμμι (= εἰμί), "be".

2. Sappho is consumed by lovesickness as she watches her beloved, who is about to be married, sitting beside the bridegroom.

1. κῆνος: Lesbian for ἔκεινος.

2. ὤνηρ = ὁ ἄνηρ.

3. ἰσδάνει = ἰζάνει. — φωνείσας, like γελαίσας in line 5, is the genitive singular of the present participle, depending on ὑπακούει. Both participles are followed by 'inner' or 'adverbial' accusatives, ἆδυ and ἰμέροεν respectively.

5. τό: demonstrative used for relative; it agrees with the inner object of γελαίσας. — ἦ μάν: a formula of asseveration.

6. καρδίαν is an accusative which more closely limits με.

7. βροχέως: Aeolic for βραχέως. — φώνας is a partitive genitive depending on οὐδέν.

9. κάμ: κατά (after apocope and assimilation). It is used adverbially with ϝέαγε, which is the second perfect of ἄγνυμι. — λέπτον: 'subtle', agreeing with πῦρ.

10. χρῷ: construe the dative with ὑπα of ὑπαδεδρόμηκεν: 'beneath my skin'. — ὑπαδεδρόμηκεν: a perfect formed from the root δρομ, which is visible in δρόμος (compare ἔδραμον).

11. ὀππάτεσσι = ὄμμασι. — ἐπιρρόμβεισι: third person plural of ἐπιρρόμβημι, Aeolic for ἐπιρρομβέω: 'make a whirring noise'.

13. κάδ is κατά; so is κακ- of κακχέεται: "Sweat pours down over me."

14. παῖσαν = πᾶσαν. — ἄγρει, from ἀγρέω, 'seizes'. — χλωροτέρα δὲ ποίας: Mediterranean peoples turn green when blood leaves their faces, as northern Europeans turn pale.

15. ὀλίγω: genitive, with ἐπιδεύης, 'lacking'. Words signifying fulness and want take the genitive.

17. ἐπεί κεν ᾖ τά: 'since these things are so'. Here the poem breaks off.

4. (Sapphic metre.)

2. ἀπυκρύπτοισι is for ἀποκρύπτουσι.

3. ὄπποτα: Aeolic for ὁπότε. — πλήθοισα: Aeolic for πλήθουσα, 'being full'.

5. (Sapphic metre.)

6. ἄλσος: a grove or 'precinct' sacred to a god or hero.

7. μαλίαν: 'of apple trees' (genitive plural). — ἔνι = ἔνεισι.

8. λιβανώτῳ: 'with frankincense'.

9. ἐν: adverbial, 'therein'. — ὔσδων is Aeolic for ὄζων.

10. ϝρόδοισι = ῥόδοις. — παῖς is Aeolic for πᾶς.

12. κατέρρει: 'comes down'.

13. ἐν: as in line 9.

14. ἄνητοι: elsewhere this word is always neuter, ἄνητον (or ἄνηθον), 'anise' or 'dill'.

15. μέλλιχα πνέοισιν: 'breathe a sweet smell'. μέλλιχα is the 'inner' accusative.

17. Κύπρι: Cypris is Aphrodite.

20. οἰνοχόεισα: feminine present participle of οἰνοχόημι (= οἰνοχοέω).

27a. This poem uses the device, "Some say this is the fairest thing in the world, and some say that; but *I* say . . ."

(Sapphic metre.)

1. ἰππήων: 'of horsemen'. In early Greek, the stems of common nouns in -ευς like ἱππεύς end in η. — στρότον: Aeolic for στρατόν. — πέσδων: Aeolic has σδ instead of ζ.

2. φαῖσι = φασί.

3. κῆν’ = ἔκεινο. — ὄττω = ὁτοῦ; ἐράω takes the genitive.

5. σύνετον: 'understandable'. — πόησαι = ποιῆσαι. The diphthong οι tends to be shortened because of the succeeding long vowel.

6. πάντι: 'to everyone'. She would have succeeded better, at least so far as we are concerned, if the papyrus on which our text is based were not so poorly preserved; but her train of thought is still reasonably clear: the case of Helen illustrates the overpowering force of love, because the minute she set eyes on Paris nothing else mattered to her — neither husband, nor parents, nor children. — περσκέθοισα: 'surpassing'. Aeolic aorist participle of περίεχω = ὑπέρεχω.

7. κάλλος: limiting accusative, 'in point of beauty'. — ἀνθρώπων is governed by the περί (in meaning equivalent to ὑπέρ) of περσκέθοισα. — τὸν ἄνδρα: Menelaus, according to this reconstruction of the poem.

8. πρῶλιπ' a contraction of προ-έλιπε.

9. ὡς is for ὥστε: 'so that the sometime majesty of Troy was ruined'.

10. κωὐδέ = καὶ οὐδέ, 'and. . . neither'. — παῖδος: one is reminded of someone.

11. ἐμνάσθη: Aeolic aorist passive of μιμνήσκω: 'she was reminded', hence 'she remembered'.

12. αὔτικ' ἴδοισαν: 'the minute she saw him', that is, Paris; but we do need some specific mention of him, so that this reconstruction of the missing text isn't quite satisfactory.

14. πτόησιν: from πτόημι (= πτοέω).

15. ὅς refers to Πόθος, 'longing' or 'desire' personified. — ὀνέμναισ' is Aeolic for ἀνέμνησε, 'put me in mind of'.

17. τᾶς is the demonstrative used instead of the relative. — βολλοίμαν (Aeolic for βουλοίμην) is a potential optative, 'I should prefer', contingent on the unexpressed condition, 'if I had my choice'. — βᾶμα: for βῆμα, 'step'.

18. ἀμάρυγμα is used of any quick, sparkling motion. — ἴδην depends on βολλοίμαν, not on λάμπρον. — προσώπω: genitive singular.

19. κἀν = καὶ ἐν.

20. πεσδομάχεντας: supply ἄνδρας. The last two lines return

to the comparison with which the poem begins, and so complete its pattern.

40. This isolated and most beautiful line is preserved for us because of the accident that its metre was of interest to an ancient writer on prosody. It consists of two introductory syllables, (which may be either short or long), then three dactyls, and finally a cretic, $- \cup -$.

$$\overline{\cup}\ \overline{\cup}: \quad -\cup\cup \quad -\cup\cup \quad -\cup\cup \quad -\cup-.$$

1. ποτά is Aeolic for ποτέ.

41. Metre: as in fragment 40. These may be two lines from the same poem.

1. ἄχαρις: 'immature'.

50. Metre: as in fragment 40.

51. Metre: two indeterminate syllables, three dactyls, and a spondee.

1. πεδά is Aeolic for μετά. — πεπτερύγωμαι is the Aeolic perfect of πτερυγόομαι, 'fly'.

55. The marriage of Hector and Andromache. (Metre: as in fragment 40).

55a. 5. A herald announces to the Trojans the arrival of Hector and Andromache. — ἄγοισι: Aeolic for ἄγουσι. — ἐλικώπιδα agrees with 'Ανδρομάχαν (line 7).

6. In the *Iliad* Thebe was Andromache's home, and Placus the mountain nearby. — ἀϊννάω: Aeolic genitive singular of ἀέναος, 'everlasting'.

8. ἐλίγματα: 'bracelets'. — κάμματα: crasis of καὶ ἔμματα (Aeolic for εἴματα, 'garments').

9. τρόνα is for θρόνα, which were embroideries of flowers or other patterns upon cloth. — An ἄθυρμα is anything in which one takes delight.

10. ἐλέφαις: Aeolic for ἐλέφας, ivory. (Since the case of

ἐλέφαις is nominative, the other items on the list of wedding-presents are presumably nominatives too, so that we should understand "and there are . . ." rather than "and they brought . . ."

11. πάτηρ φίλος: Priam.

12. φίλοις is the Aeolic accusative plural — a 'terminal' accusative used without a preposition to signify the end of the motion implied in ἦλθε: 'the report *reached* their friends'.

13. σατίναις: 'chariots'. σατίναις, ἐντρόχοις, and in the next line αἰμιόνοις (= ἡμιόνους) are all accusative.

14. παῖς is Aeolic for πᾶς.

15. παρθενίκαν: 'maidens', (genitive plural). — ἄμα is adverbial, 'all together'.

16. Περάμοιο: Aeolic for Πριάμοιο.

17. ἵπποις: again the accusative.

55c. They sing the paean.

1. ὀνεμείχνυντο: Aeolic imperfect passive of ἀναμίγνυμι: 'were mingled'.

2. ἐλέλυσδον: (σδ for ξ), 'shouted ἐλελεῦ'.

3–4. ἐπήρατον ἴαχον ὄρθιον πάον': 'raised the loud lovely paean'. ὄρθιος means 'high and clear'; and the paean (πάονα is a contraction in Aeolic of παιάϝονα) was a hymn sung to Apollo, which had the refrain ἰὴ παιάν.

4. ὀνκαλέοντες: ὀν- for ἀνα-.

5. ὕμνην: 3rd person plural imperfect: 'they praised'. — θεοεικέλοις: accusative plural.

58. To an uneducated woman. (Metre, greater Asclepiadean; cf. Alcaeus 97.)

2. οὐ πεδέχεις: 'you have no share'. πεδά is Aeolic for μετά.

3. Πιερίας: Pieria, at the foot of Mt. Olympus, was the birthplace of the Muses. — κῆν = καὶ ἐν, 'even in'. — ἀφάνης: 'obscure'.

88. A night festival.

Metre: ionic a majore followed by three trochees,

$$- - \cup\cup \quad - \cup - \cup - \bar{\cup}.$$

93. Metre: two ionic measures a majore, and a double trochee:

$$- - \cup\cup \quad - - \cup\cup \quad - \cup - \bar{\cup}.$$

3. μάτεισαι: present participle of μάτημι = πατέω, 'tread on'.

94. Metre: $\bar{\cup} - \cup\cup \quad - \cup - -$.

96. Metre: a strophe made up of two glyconic lines

$$- \bar{\cup} \quad - \cup\cup - \quad \cup -$$
$$- \bar{\cup} \quad - \cup\cup - \quad \cup -$$

and a third line which resembles the scheme of fragment 40, but has two dactyls instead of three:

$$- \bar{\cup} \quad - \cup\cup \quad - \cup\cup \quad - \cup -.$$

2. τεθνάκην: Aeolic perfect infinitive of θνήσκω.

3. ψισδομένα πόλλα: 'with many tears'. — κατελίμπανεν = κατέλειπε.

5. ὦμ' = οἴμοι.

6. ἦ μάν: 'truly'. — ἀέκοισ' = ἄκουσα.

9. μέμναισ' = μέμνησο, 'remember', (with the genitive). — πεδήπομεν: Aeolic imperfect of μεθέπω.

10. ἀλλά introduces the apodosis paratactically: 'but if not . . . but then I wish to remind you'.

11. ὄμμναισαι: Aeolic for ἀναμνῆσαι. — λάθεαι: from λήθω.

13. πόλλοις and στεφάνοις are accusative. So are πόλλαις in line 16, πλέκταις in line 17, and πεποημμέναις in line 18.

14. ϝρόδων = ῥόδων. — ὖμοι is Aeolic for ὁμοῦ. — κρόκιον is presumably a diminutive of κρόκος; but since this diminutive is unattested elsewhere, the restoration of κρόκιον here is not entirely convincing.

16. ὑπαθύμιδας: 'necklaces' of flowers.

20. βρενθείῳ: 'costly'.

98. To Atthis, reminding her of a girl who had loved her, but who has now gone away to Sardis. This poem is written in strophes of three lines each; the first line is a cretic, $- \cup -$, followed by a glyconic; the second line is a simple glyconic; and the third is a glyconic followed by a bacchius, $\cup - -$.

$$- \cup - \quad \overline{\cup}\,\overline{\cup} \quad - \cup \cup - \cup -$$
$$\overline{\cup}\,\overline{\cup} \quad - \cup \cup - \cup -$$
$$\overline{\cup}\,\overline{\cup} \quad - \cup \cup - \cup - \quad \cup - -\,.$$

2. τυῖδε: 'hither'. — νῶν: Aeolic contraction of νόον.

3. ὠς: 'when'. — πεδεζώομεν: πεδά = μετά. — βεβάως: 'firmly'.

4. ϝικέλαν = ἰκέλαν. — ἀριγνώτᾳ: 'manifest', to human sight.

8. After σελάννα supply ἐμπρέπεται from line 6.

9. περρέχοισα = ὑπερέχονσα.

9–14. The simile is continued, ostensibly in the Homeric fashion, but one perceives that the details are chosen for their emotional value to Sappho and Atthis — it is because both sea and land separate them from the girl in Sardis that the moon (which is like her beauty) 'spreads its light over the salt sea and the flowery meadows'. As the simile continues, we find ourselves accepting the picture it draws as the actual scene of the poem: Sappho and Atthis are watching the full moon rise from across the sea in Asia Minor, and its beauty reminds them of their friend. In the last strophe (if it is anything like correctly restored) the idea that the poem has a definite scene is more explicitly conveyed, because there she says, 'Our friend calls to us, but the many-eared night does not convey her voice to us across the sea', a verse which fairly demands that we picture them looking out across the sea at night.

11. πολυανθέμοις ἀρούραις: accusatives.

12. τεθάλαισι: Aeolic third person plural, perfect, of θάλλω: 'they flourish', 'they revive'.

13. ἄνθρυσκα: 'chervil'.

15. ζαφοίταισα: Aeolic present participle of διαφοιτάω. It

will be observed that Aeolic uses ζ only when confusion will result from doing so.

16–17. φρένα is in parallel construction with κῆρ, and ἱμέρῳ with ἄσᾳ: 'she is weighed down in her mind with longing, and in her heart with sorrow'. — βόρηται: Aeolic for βαρεῖται.

18. κήθυ = ἐκεῖσε, 'thither'. — ἔλθην = ἐλθεῖν. — ἄμμε = ἡμᾶς. — ὄξυ: adverbial accusative. — τά: demonstrative, referring to the 'inner' object of βόᾳ, 'what she shouts', 'her words'.

19. νῶν: 'to us'. (The dual is not used anywhere else by Sappho or Alcaeus.) — τἄπυστα is certainly difficult (the papyrus text of this strophe is very faint); presumably it stands for τὰ ἄπυστα, 'things unperceived', but at best is redundant, and moreover has to be taken parenthetically, since οὐ evidently negates the main verb, γαρύει. — νὺξ πολύως: 'night with many ears'.

20. γαρύει: Aeolic for γηρύει, 'utter'. — δι᾽ ἅλος πόρων: 'over the paths of the sea'.

107. Lament for Adonis. (Lamentation for Adonis, the young consort of Aphrodite, was ritual, like the 'song of fair Linus' in Homer.) The metre consists of two introductory syllables, two choriambs, and an Adonic (— ∪ ∪ — ∪):

ᴗ̄ ᴗ̄ — ∪ ∪ — — ∪ ∪ — — ∪ ∪ — ∪.

1. κυθέρηα, 'Cythereia', a designation of Aphrodite.

114. Metre: ∪ — ∪ — ∪ — — | ∪ ∪ — ∪ — ∪ — —.

1. γλύκηα = γλυκεῖα.
2. ϝραδίναν = ῥαδίνην.

116–128. *Fragments from the epithalamia.*

116. Sung by the bridesmaids in praise of the bride, pointing out that she was hard to get. (Dactylic hexameter.)

1. ὔσδῳ = ὄζῳ, 'bough'.
2. λελάθοντο: reduplicated second aorist of λανθάνω. — μαλοδρόπηες: 'apple-pickers' (μῆλον and δρέπω).

117. The bridesmaids complain of the brutality of the groom. (Dactylic hexameter.)

2. τε: this is the generalizing τε, used by Homer; not a conjunction.

120. To the evening star.

(Metre: line 1 is dactylic hexameter; the rest is somehow jumbled and will not scan.)

1. Αὔως = Ἠώς.

2. φέρεις ἄπυ μάτερι παῖδα: (ἄπυ is adverbial). Perhaps, 'you bring back the child to its mother', as you bring back the flocks at nightfall; but if this is part of a wedding song, we should understand, 'but you take away (φέρεις ἄπυ) the child from its mother' — another insincere complaint from the bridesmaids, as in Catullus' epithalamium, 62, 20f., where the girls address reproaches to Hesperus, "qui natam possis complexu avellere matris . . ."

121. Metre, dactylic:

$$- \cup : - \cup \cup \; - \cup \cup \; - \cup \cup \; - -.$$

This fragment was translated by Ben Jonson, 'The dear glad angel of the spring, the nightingale.'

123. Metre, dactylic, with a refrain.

$$- - \quad - \cup \cup \quad - -$$
$$- : - \cup \cup \quad - \cup \cup \quad - -$$
$$- : - \cup \cup \quad - \cup \cup \quad - -$$
$$- : - \cup \cup \quad - \cup \cup \quad - -$$

1. ἴψοι = ὑψοῦ.

3. ἀέρρατε: Aeolic aorist imperative of ἀείρω.

5. Ἄρευι: Aeolic dative of Ἄρης.

7. μεγάλω: genitive singular. — μέσδων = μείζων.

124. At the expense of the doorkeeper, who was a friend of the bridegroom posted at the door of the bedchamber. The bridesmaids pretended to try to rescue the bride, and when they failed, they revenged themselves by making fun of the doorkeeper.

Metre, dactylic.

$$\cup - \ -\cup\cup \ -\cup\cup \ --$$
$$\cup\cup \ -\cup\cup \ -\cup\cup \ --$$
$$-- \ -\cup\cup \ -\cup\cup \ --$$

1. θυρώρῳ: 'doorkeeper'. — ἐπτορόγυιοι: 'seven fathoms long'.

2. σάμβαλα: Aeolic for σάνδαλα. — πεμπεβόηα: Aeolic for πεντεβόεια: 'made of five bulls' hides'.

3. πίσυγγοι: 'shoemakers'. — ἐξεπόναισαν: Aeolic for ἐξε-πόνησαν.

127. The bridesmaids address the groom with civility.
Metre, dactylic:

$$\cup - \ -\cup\cup \ -\cup\cup \ -\cup\cup \ --$$
$$-- \ -\cup\cup \ -\cup\cup \ -\cup\cup \ --$$

1. τίῳ: Lesbian for τίνι.

2. ὄρπακι: 'sapling'. — ϝραδίνῳ = ῥαδίνῳ.

128. Congratulations to the bridegroom.
Metre: $-\cup\cup \ \ -\cup-\overline{\cup} \ | -\cup\cup \ \ -\cup-\overline{\cup}.$

1. ἄραο is second person singular, imperfect of ἄραμαι = ἀράομαι, 'prayed'.

3. ὄππατα: Aeolic for ὄμματα.

137. Metre: two introductory syllables, two dactyls, and a cretic.

$$\overline{\cup}\,\overline{\cup} \ \ -\cup\cup \ \ -\cup\cup \ \ -\cup-.$$

1. δηὖτε = δὴ αὖτε.

2. γλυκύπικρον: 'bitter-sweet'. — ὄρπετον is related to ἔρπω, and means anything that creeps.

149. A dialogue. (Alcaic metre.)

4. ἐκύκα: 'brew', hence 'prepare'.

6. τῶ: genitive singular.

152. Her daughter Cleis.
Metre: trochaic: $-\cup-\cup \ \ -\cup-- \ | -\cup-\cup \ \ --.$

IBYCUS was born at Rhegium in south Italy early in the sixth century B.C. As a young man he wrote choral narrative poems like those of Stesichorus, who was his older contemporary; but when he was driven out of Rhegium in the course of the political dissensions which took place there about the middle of the century, he took refuge at the court of Polycrates, tyrant of Samos, where he abandoned his earlier style, and turned to writing in a sophisticated, courtly style which was more appropriate to his new surroundings. The longest fragments of his work which we have are from this period.

6. Metre: generally, dactylic lines terminating in a cretic; but lines 7 and 12 are like the last line of an Alcaic stanza.

1. Κυδώνιαι μαλίδες: 'quince-trees'. μαλίς is Doric for μηλέα.
2. ῥόαι: 'pomegranate-trees'.
3. Παρθένων κᾶπος: 'the garden of the nymphs'.
7. κατάκοιτος: 'at rest'. Ibycus' passion is not like the blossoming of fruit-trees in spring, but like a tempest, violent and likely to come in any season.
10. ἀζαλέαις: 'cruel', or perhaps 'scorching'.
11. ἀθαμβής: 'shameless'.

7. Growing old he feels himself falling in love, and dreads it. (Metre, dactylic.)

4. Κύπριδι: 'for the sake of Cypris'.

ANACREON of Teos was another poet who adorned the court of Polycrates. He was born about 572 B.C. in Asia Minor. When his home was threatened by the Medes under Harpagus in 545 he fled to Abdera in Thrace; but shortly afterwards he was invited by Polycrates to Samos, where his elegant, frivolous and witty love-poetry enjoyed a great vogue. After the death of Polycrates he went to Athens, and there spent his last days, still devoted to wine, women and song.

2. To Dionysus: a prayer for the favor of Cleobulus.
Metre, glyconic strophe. The glyconic line consists of a

choriamb, $- \cup \cup -$, preceded by a trochee, $- \cup$, and followed by an iamb, $\cup -$.

$$- \bar{\cup} \quad - \cup \cup - \quad \cup -$$

The pherecratic line is like the glyconic except that after the choriamb comes — instead of $\cup -$.

$$- \bar{\cup} \quad - \cup \cup - \quad -.$$

A glyconic strophe consists of several glyconic lines followed by a pherecratic.

1. 'ναξ = ἄναξ.
3. πορφυρέη: 'rosy'.
7. κεχαρισμένης: 'acceptable'.
9. γενεῦ: Ionic second aorist imperative.
11. Δεύννσε: Ionic for Διόνυσε.

4. Metre, glyconic strophe.

1. παρθένιον βλέπων: παρθένιον is 'inner' accusative, 'looking a maiden's look'.

5. Metre, glyconic strophe.

1–2. σφαίρῃ βάλλων: 'throwing a ball'; in later verse Eros might have shot an arrow instead — the idea is the same.

3. νήνῖ = νήνυι = νεήνυι = νεᾱνιδι.

5. ἐστὶν γὰρ ἀπ' ἐυκτίτου Λέσβου: one just sees him saying this, with an insinuating smirk.

8. ἄλλην τινά undoubtedly means 'another girl'. — χάσκει: a brutal word, 'gapes'. Not a pleasant poem.

34. ἀστραγάλαι: 'dice'. — κυδοιμοί: 'tumults'.

39. A timid girl.

Metre: Ionic a minore, $\cup \cup -- \quad \underline{\cup \cup --} \quad \cup \cup --$; but the syllables indicated by the bracket *may* have their quantities interchanged — the second line of this fragment, for instance, is scanned $\cup \cup - \cup \quad - \cup -- \quad \cup \cup --$.

44. Metre: as in fragment 39.
1. ἡμίν: poetic for ἡμῖν.

4. πάρα: adverbial, with ἐστί understood.

7. ἀνασταλύζω: 'lament'.

9. 'Αΐδεω: scanned ∪ ∪ —.

11. ἑτοῖμον: supply ἐστί: 'it is certain'.

88. Metre, trochaic.

1. λοξόν: inner accusative.

2. με: subject of εἰδέναι. — σοφόν: 'clever'.

3. The first τοι is the particle; the second is the pronoun.

6. ἱπποπείρην: 'driver'. — ἐπεμβάτην: 'charioteer'.

SIMONIDES of Ceos (556–467 B.C.), like Anacreon and Ibycus, was a court poet, for he spent most of his long life in centers of wealth and power — in Athens at the court of the Peisistratids; in Thessaly at that of the Scopads; again in Athens during the first quarter of the fifth century, where he was on intimate terms with most of the leading citizens, but particularly with Themistocles; and in his extreme old age in Sicily, at the courts of Hieron of Syracuse and Theron of Acragas. But he was a man of far more energy of mind than either Ibycus or Anacreon, and (though he too could be gay and playful) a far more serious poet. He was famous in antiquity as a wise man and a great master of poignancy and pathos.

4. A scolion, or song sung at a banquet, addressed to Scopas of Thessaly. Scopas had quoted to Simonides a remark of Pittacus of Mitylene, "It is a hard thing to be a good man (ἀνὴρ ἀγαθός)," hoping no doubt that Simonides would make the flattering reply, "Yes, but you, Scopas, have succeeded." Instead Simonides replied with this scolion. In the first strophe, of which only the beginning is preserved, he recapitulated the opinion of Pittacus; in the second strophe he proceeded to criticize it, pointing out that the traditional ideal of the ἀνὴρ ἀγαθός was not difficult but impossible to attain unless one was always

fortunate; for the ἀνὴρ ἀγαθός was supposed to be not only just, brave, and generous, but also well-born, handsome, and rich. It follows that no one by his own efforts alone can be ἀγαθός, and even if a man is ἀγαθός at one time, he is always in danger of becoming κακός if his luck should change. Simonides refuses to regard the old aristocratic conception of the ἀνὴρ ἀγαθός as a valid ethical ideal. A god, he says, might perhaps be ἀγαθός, for the gods are always fortunate; but human prosperity is so insecure, and we are so little able to command it, that no man can properly be called ἀγαθός, and if he were, it would be more his good luck than his deserving.   **55979**

Metrical scheme:

1. $- \cup \cup - \quad \cup \cup - \cup \quad - \cup - -.$

2. $\cup \cup - - +$ a glyconic.

3. a glyconic $+ \cup - \cup -.$

4. $\cup \cup - \cup - +$ a glyconic.

5. a glyconic.

6. $\cup \cup - \cup - \quad - \cup - \cup \cup -.$

7. $\cup - \cup - \quad - \cup - \cup \cup -.$

8. $\cup - - \quad \cup - -.$

9. pherecratic.

10. $- \cup - \cup - -.$

3. τετράγωνον: 'foursquare'. So far the opinion of Pittacus.

11. οὐδέ μοι ἐμμελέως: 'not harmoniously with my opinion'. — τὸ Πιττάκειον νέμεται: 'this remark of Pittacus wins assent' (or 'is assented to'). νέμεται = νομίζεται; and both are related to νόμος, 'custom', 'what is regarded as right'.

12. καίτοι = καίπερ, 'although'.

14. τοῦτο γέρας: viz., to be ἐσθλός.

15. ἔστι = ἔξεστι, 'it is possible'.

17–18. 'For while he is prosperous every man is ἀγαθός, but κακός if things go wrong in any way'.

19. κἀπί = καὶ ἐπί. ἐπὶ πλεῖστον, 'for the most part'. — After ἄριστοι supply εἰσίν.

20. οὕς κε θεοὶ φιλῶσιν: 'those whom the gods love', that is, those who are the most fortunate.

21-22. τὸ μὴ γενέσθαι δυνατὸν διζήμενος: 'searching for something that can't occur'. γενέσθαι is an epexegetic or explanatory infinitive depending on δυνατόν.

22-23. κενεὰν μοῖραν αἰῶνος βαλέω: 'spend an unprofitable portion of my life'. — ἐς ἄπρακτον ἐλπίδα: 'on an impossible hope'.

24. πανάμωμον ἄνθρωπον is in apposition with ἐλπίδα. The ὅσοι clause emphasizes the rarity of this 'altogether unexceptionable man, among all of us who reap the fruit of the solidly founded earth'.

26. 'But if I should find him I'll let you know'. Suave irony.

27-40. Now Simonides sets up a more modest ideal, and describes the sort of man he approves.

27. ἐπαίνημι: The mixture of dialects which the later choral poets cultivated is aptly illustrated here: side by side are the Aeolic ἐπαίνημι and the Ionic φιλέω.

28. ἑκών, which belongs to the ὅστις clause, is made very emphatic by being put first. Simonides' judgment of a man depends on his voluntary actions, not on his appearance or his family or any other accidental circumstance.

29-30. But one might be compelled, against his will, to do something αἰσχρόν.

34. κακός: this time in its moral sense. — ἀπάλαμνος: 'inept'.

37-38. τῶν γὰρ ἠλιθίων ἀπείρων γενέθλα: 'for the race of fools is innumerable'. He makes good sense a condition of virtue, since without it a man can't choose intelligently between good actions and bad.

5. The bodies of those who fell at Thermopylae were buried there, but at Sparta there was dedicated to them a sacred enclosure containing an altar, upon which offerings were made to

them. This poem must have been sung at the shrine in Sparta, perhaps when it was dedicated.

Metre, dactylic, varied with epitrites ($-\smile--$) and trochaic sequences.

2. εὐκλεὴς μὲν ἀ τύχα: He doesn't say that they had good fortune, but that their fortune gave them fame.

3. This precinct is a cenotaph; so, 'For a tomb they have an altar, instead of mourning they have remembrance, instead of pity praise'. The τάφος could only be where they were buried, and the γόος would be made over the corpse itself.

4. ἐντάφιον may mean 'winding-sheet', or possibly 'offerings' to the dead.

5. Another οὔτε should be understood before εὐρώς. It is actually in the manuscript, but it disturbs the metre, and for reasons of style Simonides would have been likely to leave it out. — πανδμάτωρ = πανδαμάτωρ, 'all-subduing'.

6. 'But these brave men's holy precinct has won as its indwelling protector (οἰκέταν) the good report that is theirs in Greece'.

7. Leonidas is a witness because he had a special shrine nearby.

8–9. The κόσμον ἀρετῆς he bestowed upon his country; the κλέος he enjoys himself.

6. Metre: 1. two choriambs, two dactyls, one cretic;
     2. three choriambs, one iamb;
     3. three dactyls, one cretic;
     4. trochaic.

When the roof of Scopas' great hall fell in (Simonides being providentially absent), Scopas and his whole family were killed. The disaster seems to have made a deep impression on Simonides, and these lines are part of a dirge which he wrote for those who lost their lives in it.

1. φάσῃς: Doric aorist subjunctive of φημί, in a negative command.

3. οὐδέ: 'not even'. —μνίας can be scanned as two longs, but the diphthong υι could easily be shortened before the succeeding long vowel; then the line would have a metrical pattern resembling that of Sappho's dactylic lines, which end with a cretic.

7. Heracles, for instance, was a type of the laboring demigod, and Achilles never reached old age.

8. Metre, dactylic; but the first foot of line 1 is a trochee.
1. δασπλῆτα, 'dread to approach', is related to πελάζω. — μίαν Χάρυβδιν: 'the same Charybdis'.

9. Metre: 1. pherecratic; — — — ∪ ∪ — —;
       2. epitrite, hemiepes, epitrite, hemiepes:
       3. ∪ ∪ : — ∪ ∪ — ∪,
                    hemiepes (— ∪ ∪ — ∪ ∪ —);
       4. — : — ∪ ∪ — ∪,
                    hemiepes (— ∪ ∪ — ∪ ∪ —);
       5. — : — ∪ ∪ — . . . .

The element — ∪ ∪ — ∪ of lines 3 and 4 consumes the same time as an epitrite, and may have been regarded as equivalent; or it may be simply an Adonic.

3. ὅμως: 'nevertheless', no matter what we do.
4. κείνου: i.e., death.

13. Danae and the infant Perseus are adrift at sea in the carved chest.
3. τέτμε is from the epic verb ἔτετμον, 'overtook', 'reached'.
4. λίμνα is subject, along with ἄνεμος.
5. ἤριπεν: an intransitive aorist of ἐρείπω; 'she swooned'. — οὔ τ' ἀδιάντοισι παρειαῖς: 'and with cheeks not unwet'.
8. ἀωτεῖς: 'sleep'.
10. δούρατι: 'craft', 'boat'.
11. νυκτιλαμπεῖ κυανέῳ τε δνόφῳ: 'in the gloom, illumined by night (i.e. not very much), and dark'.
19. μεταβουλία: 'change of intention'. Presumably Zeus has

willed this catastrophe for Danae, but she prays that he will change his mind.

48. Cleobulus of Lindos had written a poem on the tomb of Midas. The tomb was surmounted by a bronze statue of a maiden, who is the speaker of Cleobulus' poem: "A bronze maiden am I, and I lie on Midas' tomb. So long as water runs and tall trees grow, and the sun shines when he rises and the splendid moon, and the rivers flow and the sea surges, I remaining here upon this much-wept tomb shall say to those who pass by that Midas is buried here." Here is Simonides' rejoinder.

Metre: dactylic, varied with epitrites ($- \cup - -$), and ending with a trochaic sequence.

1. $- \cup - - \quad - \cup \cup - \cup \cup - - \quad - \cup \cup - \cup \cup - -;$
2. $- \cup \cup - \cup \cup - \quad - \cup \cup - \cup \cup -;$
3. $- \cup \cup \quad - \cup \cup \quad - \cup \cup \quad - \cup \cup \quad - -;$
4. $- \cup - \cup \quad - \cup - - \quad - \cup \cup - \cup \cup -;$
5. $- -;$
6. $\cup : \quad - \cup \cup - \cup \cup - - \quad - \cup - -;$
7. $- \cup \cup - \cup \cup - - \quad - \cup - - \quad - \cup - \cup - -.$

1. νόῳ πίσυνος qualifies τίς: 'Who that relied on his intelligence . . . ?'

2. ποταμοῖσι, ἄνθεσι, κτλ.: the datives depend on ἀντία in line 4.

3. Both ἀελίου and σελάνας depend on φλογί.

4. θέντα: (agreeing with Κλεόβουλον) 'when he reckons'. ἀντία (neuter plural) is adverbial, 'against'.

5. στάλας: this word is isolated metrically in such a way as to make it ring with scathing contempt.

7. θραύοντι: Doric for θραύουσι.

83. On the seer Megistias, who foresaw his death before Thermopylae, but refused to abandon the army. (Elegiac metre.)

1. Μεγιστία: Doric genitive of Megistias.

3. μάντιος is in apposition with Μεγιστία.

84. To Callias, on the death of his friend Megacles.

85. On Archedice, who was the daughter of Hippias, tyrant of Athens.

1. ἀριστεύω means 'excel', 'be eminent'. — τῶν ἐφ' ἑαυτοῦ: 'among the men of his time'.

2. Ἱππίου Ἀρχεδίκην: 'Archedice, daughter of Hippias'.

3. πατρός is a genitive of source, and her other relatives fall into the same construction.

88. 1. προμαχοῦντες: 'champions'. — χρυσοφόρων: a slur on the rich costume of the Persians.

91. Inscription at Thermopylae.

1. τέτορες: 'four' (Doric).

92. On the dead at Thermopylae.

1. ἀγγέλλειν: infinitive for imperative, a military use.

2. ῥήμασι: 'words', 'precepts'. They had acted as Spartans were brought up to act.

105. King Pausanias caused this arrogant couplet to be inscribed on the golden tripod which was made out of a tithe of the Persian spoils and dedicated by the Greeks to Apollo at Delphi. Great anger resulted, and the words were erased and in their stead were inscribed the names of the Greek cities which had taken part in the battle of Plataea.

118. On the Athenian dead at Plataea.

3. περιθεῖναι: 'to put (like a wreath) around'.

4. χρώμενοι: 'enjoying'.

121. On the Lacedaemonian dead at Plataea.

135. 4. ἤμπλακες: 'you missed'. Verbs of aiming at, hitting, etc., take the genitive.

138. Brotachus of Gortyn.

"Phlebas the Phoenician, a fortnight dead,
Forgot the cry of gulls and the long sea swell
And the profit and loss."

(T. S. Eliot, *The Waste Land*)

142. On the hound Lycas.

2. ἴσκω: 'I think'.

4. οἰονόμοι: 'solitary'.

PINDAR of Thebes (518–446 B.C.) came of the proudest aristocracy of his city; by temperament and conviction he was one of the true Bourbons of all time. He believed that the usages and customs of his noble contemporaries were intimately bound up with Apollo and the Graces and the whole company of Heaven; for 'baser' men he had no regard. In manner he was haughty and imperious, in style sudden, oracular and splendid. He felt that he was a great poet by nature, and had nothing but contempt for those who learned their art. He wrote all kinds of choral poems — hymns, paeans, dirges, hyporchemes, dithyrambs, processional odes; a few only of these survive in fragments. But forty-four of his poems in a strange and special form have been preserved — the epinikion, or victory-song sung to celebrate success at the sacred games which were held at Olympia, Pytho, Nemea and the Isthmus. That victory in these games was highly prized and much sought after we have seen — the glamor of the victory never left the man who had won it. Moreover, this glamor was not like the ordinary prestige which attends success in other endeavors — it was felt to be half-divine. Olympia was a holy precinct of Zeus; the games held there were acts of worship, in which Zeus was presumed to take delight, no less than in a hymn or sacrifice; and if a man won, evidently he enjoyed the god's favor. So that to celebrate an Olympian victory by an elaborate choral dance for which an ambitious poem had been specially written was not in itself absurd. Nevertheless the composition of an epinikion was a tricky matter: it had to celebrate the victory, but not be confined to it; it had to associate the victor's triumph with a whole world of legend and heroic example. This Pindar, with great art and high seriousness, attempted to do.

Olympian XIV. For Asopichus of Orchomenos, victor in the boys' footrace, 476 B.C., at Olympia. The ode was sung on his return home, by a κῶμος or revel of his friends; they invoke the Graces, who were especially worshipped at Orchomenos.

Metrical scheme:

1. $- : - \cup \quad - \cup \cup -;$
2. $\cup : - \cup - \cup \quad - \cup \cup - \quad \cup - \cup - -;$
3. $- \cup \cup - \quad \cup - \cup - \quad \cup \cup - -;$
4. $\cup \cup \cup - \quad \cup \cup - \cup \quad - \cup - \quad \cup \cup - \cup$
$- \cup -;$
5. $- \cup \cup - \cup - \quad - \cup - \quad - \cup - \cup -;$
6. $- \cup \cup - \cup - \quad - \cup \cup -;$
7. $- \cup \cup - \cup \cup \quad - \cup - \cup \cup - -;$
8. $- \cup - - \quad - - \cup \cup - \cup -;$
9. $- \cup \cup - \quad - \cup - \quad - \cup - \cup - \quad - \cup \cup -;$
10. $- : - \cup - \cup - \quad - \cup - \quad - \cup \cup - \cup -;$
11. $- \overline{\cup \cup} \cup - \quad - - \cup -;$
12. $- \cup \cup - \cup - \cup \quad - \cup \cup - \quad \cup - \cup - -.$

1. Καφισίων ὑδάτων: the Boeotian river Cephisus. ὑδάτων is partitive genitive after λαχοῖσαν.

2. λαχοῖσαν depends on ἔδραν, and αἵτε depends on Χάριτες.

3. λιπαρᾶς: 'rich', with Ἐρχομενοῦ, which is a variant of Ὀρχομενοῦ.

4. Μινυᾶν: the Minyans were early inhabitants of this region. — ἐπίσκοποι: 'protectors'.

5–6. τὰ τερπνὰ καὶ τὰ γλυκέα were, of course, the special province of the Graces. — ἄνεται is from ἄνω, 'accomplish'.

8. οὐδέ: 'not even'.

9. κοιρανέοντι: Doric for κοιρανέουσι, 'rule over'. — ταμίαι: supply οὖσαι.

12. σέβοντι: Doric for σέβουσι.

13. Ἀγλαΐα, Εὐφροσύνα, and Θαλία are the names of the Graces.

14. θεῶν κρατίστου: Zeus.

15. ἐπᾱκοοῖτε: from an assumed verb ἐπηκοέω, 'give ear'.

16. τόνδε κῶμον: 'this revel'. — ἐπ' εὐμενεῖ τύχᾳ: 'on the occasion of their good fortune'.

17–18. τρόπῳ is the tune, and μελέταις, 'cares', refers to the verse. — ἔμολον: 'I came' — the poet speaking for himself.

19. ἁ Μινύεια: supply πόλις.

20ff. Cleodamus, the father of Asopichus, is dead; so Echo is despatched to Hades to tell him the good news.

21. Ἀχοῖ: vocative of Ἀχώ.

22. ὄφρα introduces εἴπῃς. υἱὸν εἴπῃς ὅτι . . . is equivalent to εἴπῃς ὅτι δ υἱὸς κτλ. . . . , 'tell him that his son has crowned his young locks . . .'

24. ἀέθλων πτεροῖσι: 'with feathers (or wings) of prizes'.

Isthmian VII. For Strepsiades of Thebes, victor in the pancration at the Isthmus, probably in 456 B.C. This is a poem of celebration, but also of comfort, for the young victor's uncle, who was also named Strepsiades, had been killed in battle only a short time before, fighting in defense of his city.

Metre: the strophes and antistrophes correspond exactly and are scanned as follows:

```
1. ∪∪−∪∪−∪−  ∪−−;
2. −−∪∪−∪−|∪−∪−  −∪−;
3. −:−∪−∪  −∪∪−  ∪−−;
4. −−∪∪−∪−  ∪−−;
5. −−  −∪∪−∪−|−−∪∪−∪−|
       −−∪−∪∪−|  −−∪−∪−.
```

The epodes are all alike:

```
1. −∪−∪∪−∪−  ∪−∪−;
2. −−∪∪−∪−  −∪∪−−;
3. −−∪∪−∪−;
4. ∪∪−∪∪−∪−  ∪−−;
```

5. ⏤⏤∪∪⏤∪⏤   ⏤⏤∪∪⏤∪⏤;
6. ⏤∪∪⏤   ⏤⏤;
7. ⏤⏤∪∪⏤   ⏤∪⏤∪∪⏤.

1–15. He asks Thebes which of the famous events of her history has most delighted her.

1. τίνι τῶν πάρος . . . καλῶν ἐπιχωρίων: 'because of which of the famous events of former times that happened here?' τῶν καλῶν should be taken together, with πάρος and ἐπιχωρίων as qualifiers. — Θήβα: poetic for Θῆβαι, 'Thebes'.

2–3. θυμὸν τεὸν εὔφρανας: 'did you delight your heart?'

3–5. Was it when you witnessed the birth of Dionysus?

3. ἦρα is used to mark the first of several questions. — χαλκοκρότου: 'worshipped with a clash of bronze', that is, of cymbals. — πάρεδρον depends on Διόνυσον. Dionysus is properly a πάρεδρος of Demeter, because he is the god of the vine, she of grain.

4–5. ἁνίκ᾽ ἄντειλας Διόνυσον: 'when you caused Dionysus to arise'. ἁνίκα is Doric for ἡνίκα, 'when'; ἄντειλας is the unaugmented first aorist, second person singular, of ἀνατέλλω, 'cause to arise'. Thebes in a sense caused Dionysus to arise because Semele, his mother, was a Theban princess.

5–7. Or when you received Zeus coming to beget Heracles?

5. δεξαμένα, like ἁνίκ᾽ ἄντειλας, depends on εὔφρανας, 'did you rejoice most on receiving, etc.' There seems to have been a story that when Zeus visited Alcmene there was a shower of gold; hence Zeus is said to be 'snowing with gold at midnight'. — μεσονύκτιον is equivalent to an adverb, though grammatically it agrees with Zeus, who is τὸν φέρτατον θεῶν.

6. Ἀμφιτρύωνος modifies ἄλοχον as well as θυρέτροις.

7. μετῆλθεν: 'wooed'. — Ἡρακλείοις γοναῖς: 'for the sake of Heracles' birth'.

8–10. Or did you most rejoice because of Teiresias, or Iolaus, or the dragon's teeth?

8. Τειρεσίαο (genitive singular): Teiresias the seer, who

prophesied in the reigns of Laius, Oedipus, and Creon, Kings of Thebes.

9. Iolaus was another Theban hero, a companion of Heracles.

10. 'Or because of the Sown Men, tireless with the spear?' Cadmus slew a dragon when he founded Thebes, and sowed the dragon's teeth in a field; armed men sprang up and almost exterminated each other; the few who survived were the ancestors of well-known Theban families.

10–12. Or when you repelled the attack of the Adrastus of Argos? (This is the story of the Seven against Thebes.) — καρτερᾶς ἐξ ἀλαλᾶς: 'out of the harsh tumult of battle'. — ἄμπεμψας: unaugmented aorist of ἀναπέμπω; 'you sent back'. — ὀρφανὸν μυρίων ἑτάρων: 'deprived of his countless companions'.

12–15. Or when you colonized Lacedaemon?

15. Αἰγεῖδαι: Pindar himself belonged to this family.

16–22. But enough. Ancient glories are forgotten, or remembered only if they are the themes of song. Then let us sing for Strepsiades, who has won an Isthmian victory. — Deftly he introduces the achievement of Strepsiades, not comparing it directly with the former glories of Thebes (for that would be absurd), but yet putting it in the same context.

16. ἀλλὰ γάρ: 'but stop, for . . .' — παλαιὰ εὕδει χάρις: 'ancient glory sleeps'.

17–19. 'and men are forgetful of that which does not achieve the high celebrity of song, yoked to glorious streams of words'. The metaphors are, to say the least, bold. ζυγέν was really a dead metaphor, and suggested perhaps no more than 'joined'. ἄωτος was a word of high poetic patina, signifying the choicest portion or excellence of a thing. In Homer it means the fine down of wool. — ἀμνάμονες . . . ὅ τι means 'forgetful of whatever . . .'.

20. κώμαζε: 'revel'.

21. καὶ Στρεψιάδᾳ: 'for Strepsiades too'. — φέρει νίκαν: his-

torical present, 'he has carried off a victory'. — Ἰσθμοῖ is the locative dative.

22. σθένει: dative of cause. — ἰδεῖν limits μορφάεις. — φυᾶς refers to his physical growth, his strength and good looks.

23-37. This victory also revives the memory of his uncle, who bore the same name, and who was killed fighting for his country.

23. 'He shines forth, (made famous) by music'. (The metaphor is of a torch.)

24. κοινὸν θάλος: 'a wreath of olive common to them both'.

25. ᾧ: the uncle.

26. 'But honor is laid up for brave men', though they are dead. ἀντίκειται means 'is placed opposite'. The metaphor is uncertain; perhaps we should think of a list or ledger, in which honor is placed opposite their names.

27. Join ἴστω very closely with αὔξων (line 29); the subject of ἴστω is the ὅστις clause: 'Whoever wards off the hailstorm of blood for his fatherland, let him know that he increases, etc.'

30. Join ἀπό and θανών.

31. Διοδότοιο παῖ: the elder Strepsiades.

32. αἰνέων: 'emulating'. — καὶ: 'also'.

36. ἔσχον: 'maintained'.

37-48. But now that fine weather has succeeded the storm, let us enjoy it quietly and without being ambitious, for the ambitious come to a bad end: witness Bellerophon.

38. Γαιάοχος is Poseidon.

41. ἔκαλος = ἔκηλος, 'in quiet'.

43. Some are more fortunate than others, but ambition is always a mistake. (Aristocratic quietism.)

44. βραχὺς ἐξικέσθαι: 'he is too short to reach'.

44-47. When Bellerophon tried to ascend to heaven on the back of Pegasus the winged horse, he was thrown.

46. Βελλεροφόνταν is in apposition with δεσπόταν.

48. μένει: 'awaits'. πικροτάτα τελευτά is the subject, and τὸ

παρ δίκαν γλυκύ, 'sweetness to which one is not entitled' is the object.

49–51. 'Nevertheless, Apollo, give us a crown at Pytho'. Pindar's warning is probably directed against political ambition; victory in the games was an example of worthy ambition which was not likely to bring harm.

49. Λοξία: vocative of Λοξίας, 'Apollo'.

51. καὶ Πυθόϊ: 'at Pytho too'.

64. In praise of Athens.

(This fragment is numbered 64 in C. M. Bowra's edition of Pindar, Oxford, 1935.)

Metre: 1. — : — ∪ ∪ — ∪ ∪ — ∪ ∪ — ∪ ∪ — ∪ —
　　　　　(dactylic with a cretic ending)

2. — : ∪ ∪ ∪ — — — ∪ ∪ — —
　　　(dactylic, but ∪ ∪ ∪ — — seems to be a resolved epitrite)

3. — ∪ ∪ — ∪ ∪ — —
　　　(dactylic).

1. λιπαραί: 'rich'.

SCOLIA. These were drinking-songs sung at Athens in the early part of the fifth century.

1. 1. Τριτογένεια: an epithet of Athene. It means either (1) born from Lake Tritonis in Libya; or (2) from Triton, a torrent in Boeotia; or (3) from a spring in Arcadia; or (4) from the head of Zeus; or (5) born on the third day of the month; or (6) something else.

10. This and the following scolion commemorate the assassination of Hipparchus the tyrant by the court favorites Harmodius and Aristogeiton.

1. κλαδί: dative, in place of the more usual form κλάδῳ. It was customary for the singer of a scolion to hold up a myrtle-bough while he sang; and it appears that Harmodius and Aris-

togeiton concealed their daggers under the myrtle-leaves which they wore in the Panathenaic procession.

4. This isn't true: Hippias was the reigning tyrant when his younger brother Hipparchus was killed, and he continued to rule for four years longer.

17, 18. A wish, and a reply.

18. 1. ἄπυρον: 'untouched by fire'. The word is used in Homer of tripods which are new. — χρυσίον: a golden object, but we aren't told what; perhaps a vase.

AESCHYLUS is the Athenian tragedian (525–456 B.C.).
2. On the slain in a battle in Thessaly.
2. πολύρρηνον: 'rich in flocks'.
3. On himself.
1. Εὐφορίωνος: 'son of Euphorion'.
2. καταφθίμενον agrees with Αἰσχύλον. — Γέλας: Aeschylus died in exile at Gela in Sicily. He was sitting out of doors one day when a high-flying eagle, wishing to break open a tortoise which it had just captured, and mistaking the bald head of Aeschylus for a boulder, dropped the tortoise on it; the results for Aeschylus were fatal.

PLATO. This is the Athenian philosopher (427–347 B.C.). The epigrams attributed to him are of doubtful authenticity.

4. It is said that Plato had a pupil whose name was Aster; so this epigram and the next may have been written by him.

5. To Aster dead.

10. On the Eretrians, who were carried off to Ecbatana in Media when their city was captured by the Persians in 490.